The Development of Western Civilization

Narrative Essays in the History of Our Tradition from
Its Origins in Ancient Israel and Greece to the Present

Edited by Edward W. Fox

Professor of Modern European History
Cornell University

THE AGE OF POWER

BY CARL J. FRIEDRICH
and CHARLES BLITZER

Frontispiece of the first edition of Hobbes's *Leviathan* (1651).

The Age of Power

CARL J. FRIEDRICH

HARVARD UNIVERSITY

AND

CHARLES BLITZER

SMITHSONIAN INSTITUTION

*

Cornell University Press

ITHACA AND LONDON

CORNELL UNIVERSITY PRESS

First published 1957
Tenth printing 1970

International Standard Book Number 0–8014–9843–0

PRINTED IN THE UNITED STATES OF AMERICA BY THE

VAIL-BALLOU PRESS, INC., BINGHAMTON, NEW YORK

Foreword

THE proposition that each generation must rewrite history is more widely quoted than practiced. In the field of college texts on western civilization, the conventional accounts have been revised, and sources and supplementary materials have been developed; but it is too long a time since the basic narrative has been rewritten to meet the rapidly changing needs of new college generations. In the mid-twentieth century such an account must be brief, well written, and based on unquestioned scholarship and must assume almost no previous historical knowledge on the part of the reader. It must provide a coherent analysis of the development of western civilization and its basic values. It must, in short, constitute a systematic introduction to the collective memory of that tradition which we are being asked to defend. This series of narrative essays was undertaken in an effort to provide such a text for an introductory history survey course and is being published in the present form in the belief that the requirements of that one course reflected a need that is coming to be widely recognized.

Now that the classic languages, the Bible, the great historical novels, even most non-American history, have dropped out of the normal college preparatory program, it is imperative that a text in the history of European civilization be fully self-explanatory. This means not only that it must begin at the beginning, with the origins of our civilization in ancient Israel and Greece, but that it must introduce every name or event that takes an integral place in the account and ruthlessly delete all others no matter how firmly imbedded in historical protocol. Only thus simplified and complete will the narrative present a sufficiently clear outline of those major trends and developments that have led from the beginning of our recorded time to the most pressing of our current problems. This simplification, however, need not involve intellectual dilution or evasion. On the contrary, it can effectively raise rather than lower the level of presentation. It is on this assumption that the present series has been based, and each contributor has been urged to write for a mature and literate audience. It is hoped, therefore, that the essays may also prove profitable and rewarding to readers outside the college classroom.

The plan of the first part of the series is to sketch, in related essays, the narrative of our history from its origins to the eve of the French Revolution; each is to be written by a recognized scholar and is designed to serve as the basic reading for one week in a semester course. The developments of the nineteenth and twentieth centuries will be covered in a succeeding series which will provide the same quantity of reading material for each week of the second semester. This scale of presentation has been adopted in the conviction that any understanding of the central problem of the preservation of the integrity and dignity of the individual human being depends first on an examination of the origins of our tradition in the politics and philosophy of the ancient Greeks and the religion of the ancient Hebrews and then on a relatively more detailed knowledge of its recent development within our industrial urban society.

The decision to devote equal space to twenty-five centuries and to a century and a half was based on analogy with the human memory. Those events most remote tend to be remembered in least detail but often with a sense of clarity and perspective that is absent in more recent and more crowded recollections. If the roots of our tradition must be identified, their relation to the present must be carefully developed. The nearer the narrative approaches contemporary times, the more difficult and complicated this becomes. Recent experience must be worked over more carefully and in more detail if it is to contribute effectively to an understanding of the contemporary world.

It may be objected that the series attempts too much. The attempt is being made, however, on the assumption that any historical development should be susceptible of meaningful treatment on any scale and in the realization that a very large proportion of today's college students do not have more time to invest in this part of their education. The practical alternative appears to lie between some attempt to create a new brief account of the history of our tradition and the abandonment of any serious effort to communicate the essence of that tradition to all but a handful of our students. It is the conviction of everyone contributing to this series that the second alternative must not be accepted by default.

In a series covering such a vast sweep of time, few scholars would find themselves at home thoroughly in the fields covered by more than one or two of the essays. This means, in practice, that almost every essay should be written by a different author. In spite of apparent drawbacks, this pro-

cedure promises real advantages. Each contributor will be
in a position to set higher standards of accuracy and insight
in an essay encompassing a major portion of the field of
his life's work than could ordinarily be expected in surveys
of some ten or twenty centuries. The inevitable discon-
tinuity of style and interpretation could be modified by
editorial co-ordination; but it was felt that some discon-
tinuity was in itself desirable. No illusion is more easily
acquired by the student in an elementary course, or is more
prejudicial to the efficacy of such a course, than that a single
smoothly articulated text represents the very substance of
history itself. If the shift from author to author, week by
week, raises difficulties for the beginning student, they are
difficulties that will not so much impede his progress as
contribute to his growth.

In this essay, *The Age of Power*, Mr. Carl J. Friedrich
and Mr. Charles Blitzer have produced a work as much of
synthesis as of summary. Even though the seventeenth century was, as they say, the period during which "modern
science, modern philosophy, and the modern state . . . all
emerged," it has been studied less—except in the English
field—than any other segment of European history since
the end of the Middle Ages. Comprehensive surveys of the
century have begun to appear only recently, and there are
still no generally accepted—or even widely debated—interpretations of its historical development. The authors
were, therefore, confronted with the necessity, hardly to
be expected in a series such as this, of organizing a field of
study at the same time as presenting it in a brief narrative
essay. In response, they have not only produced an ar-
resting thesis, but appropriately have traced its pattern in
the bold outlines and highlighted its structure in the chia-

roscuro that were characteristic of the baroque style, which they adopted as the symbol of this turbulent and paradoxical age.

The authors and the editor wish to express their gratitude for helpful suggestions to Mr. I. Bernard Cohen.

EDWARD WHITING FOX

Ithaca, New York
March 1957

Contents

Foreword, by Edward Whiting Fox v

I The Pattern of Politics and Economics 1

II The Baroque 20

III The Power of Mind and Spirit 39

IV The Thirty Years' War 73

V France: Absolute Power 97

VI England: Constitutional Power 119

VII Toward a New Balance of Power 150

Chronological Summary 189

Suggestions for Further Reading 193

Index 197

THE AGE OF POWER

CHAPTER I

The Pattern of Politics and Economics

IN the history of Europe, the period between the years 1610 and 1713 was a time of vast destruction, of brilliant creation—a time of change. Although it would be profoundly unhistorical to assume that the direction of this change, and its inevitability, were apparent to the actors in the drama of seventeenth-century Europe, it is clear that many of them were aware of the historical role of their age; it is no accident that the word "modern" became current in the seventeenth century. For in a very real sense the modern world as we know it is a seventeenth-century creation; modern science, modern philosophy, and the modern state, although they have roots in an earlier past, all emerged during this age. And these three great developments are, in turn, manifestations of an underlying common core. This core is the new sense of power, the power of man to shape his own society, his own destiny. In some of the key thinkers and actors of the age, this sense of power was Promethean in its limitless striving. Nature herself was disciplined by the royal will of Louis XIV (and his landscape architect, André Lenôtre) in the gardens of Versailles. Indeed, the entire universe awaited the same fate at the hands of the new sciences, which, in the words of

Francis Bacon, "extend more widely the limits of the power and greatness of man."

Power has always been one of man's dominant ends, and the search for it one of his great passions. But probably no age allowed this passion to become so all-engulfing, unless it be our own, in many ways so strangely akin to the seventeenth century. Hence Thomas Hobbes (self-styled "child of fear") in his uncompromising adulation of power coined perhaps the most revealing passage of the age: "So that in the first place, I put for a generall inclination of all mankind, a perpetuall and restless desire of Power, after Power, that ceaseth only in Death." [1] To him all passions were in the last analysis reducible to that dominant passion for power, "for Riches, Knowledge and Honour are but severall sorts of power." [2] Although the manifestations of this restless search for power are to be found in every sphere of human activity during the seventeenth century, two in particular are so central to the history of the period that we must speak of them at the very outset: mercantilism and the modern state.

Mercantilism as a System of Power

All the varied economic activities of the century were encompassed within the set of economic and political doctrines which became known as mercantilism. This complex of ideas—as its name, mercantilism, suggests—concerns methods of organizing commerce, but commerce so broadly interpreted as to include all economic activity in general. If one wants to call it a system, it was a system

[1] Thomas Hobbes, *Leviathan*, ed. by Michall Oakeshott (Oxford, 1946), pt. I, ch. xi, p. 64.
[2] *Ibid.*, pt. I, ch. viii, p. 46.

full of divergencies verging on contradictions. But the central idea was quite distinct: the state, as a secular organization, had the key role in shaping economic well-being. In this context the state was clearly understood, therefore, to have practical and expedient rather than moral objectives. Thus, in a sense, mercantilism was as much a political as an economic doctrine. It may, indeed, be called the most comprehensive theory of the emergent modern state.

The earlier mercantilists strove to increase the wealth of a nation primarily, if not exclusively, for the purpose of providing the sinews of war and conquest. In a famous letter, Jean Baptiste Colbert, Louis XIV's controller general of finance, wrote, "Trade is the source of public finance, and public finance is the vital nerve of war." And victory in war was seen in turn to be the basis for aggrandizement and power. With this objective of ultimate power clearly in mind, one can say that "national wealth through the regulation and protection of commerce" was the mercantilist credo. This regulation and protection of commerce was superimposed by an authoritarian bureaucracy, an institution which reached its greatest heights in France. So early an act as the Elizabethan Statute of Artificers (1563) clearly shows the trend which was to triumph in the next century in the policies of Richelieu, Wallenstein, Gustavus Adolphus, and Cromwell. For no matter how deeply divided politically, all the top-ranking leaders of this period were practitioners of mercantilist policy, and much of their success flowed from their superior handling and radical application of these policies.

Active governmental concern with every department of economic life was a recurrent theme of the century. The

state—the idealized embodiment of the authoritarian bureaucracy—was made into the ever-alert guardian of the
nation's entire economic life. Prosperity, therefore, was
taken to be dependent upon the exertions of a "creative
state"—a theme which has been resumed in our time. The
further notion that the gain of one state was necessarily
the loss of another inevitably contributed to a marked intensification of these efforts. In the words of Francis Bacon,
England's lord chancellor, "The increase of any estate
must be upon the foreigner, for whatsoever is somewhere
gotten is somewhere lost." Hence, in the latter half of the
century, when mercantilism was at its height, Europe experienced a succession of trade wars, starting with the
Anglo-Dutch conflict of 1653–1654.

The early mercantilists became so preoccupied with the
gathering of "treasure," more especially gold and silver,
that they laid themselves open to the charge of "cash-box
thinking." This failing, however, is understandable in
terms of the decisive effect of gold upon the fate of governments, and particularly upon the successes of the Spanish during the sixteenth century, which they had observed.
If they concentrated upon methods of acquiring gold or
its equivalents as the prince's main concern, however, their
most significant achievement was to shift their emphasis
from the physical capture of gold and other treasures to
the development of trade. Mercantilism thus came to foster
many remarkable innovations to enlarge the government's
resources—none more so than the modern state itself.

The Modern State

None of these economic doctrines viewed apart from
the background of political thought about the state is really

comprehensible. It is surely impossible to understand the disintegration of the system of government with estates without considering the economic revolution resulting from colonial enterprise. But it is equally impossible to understand the economic doctrines of mercantilism without comprehending the political thought of rising absolutism, of state and sovereignty. Advanced thought was both absolutist and mercantilist, revolving around the central idea that through appropriate legislation and policy men have the power to mold their social environment. Finally, it is difficult to understand this political thought unless it is accompanied by a brief sketch of the political evolution which it sought to rationalize and for which it set the frame.

Although it now seems perfectly clear that nothing could have been expected in 1610 but the establishment of the modern state system, many thoughtful men were then far from certain what the future held in store. The activists of the Catholic Counter Reformation were, in fact, determined, through force if necessary, to re-establish the lost unity of Christendom. Yet certainly the modern state had been in the making over a long period of time. Princes of superior ability in England and France, in Sweden and Spain, had been developing effective bureaucracies, the core of modern government. Such a great institution—and is not the modern state the greatest of them all?—"emerges" rather than is born, and by "emergence" is meant the process by which during a given period the outlines become visible to all, like a whale coming to the surface of the sea. During the fifty years between 1610 and 1660, in the period when Thomas Hobbes discoursed upon the great Leviathan and when John Lilburn (1614–1657) cried out in anguish against the new trend,[3] the modern state may be said to have emerged; the position of the state was firmly established throughout most of Europe by 1710. In 1610 the political focal point of Europe's order still seemed to be the ancient Holy Roman Empire. Even England, no less than the continent, seemed on the road to princely rule, in fact, somewhat further advanced on it; and under Paul V the papacy was earnestly at work restoring the temporal power of the Holy See, skillfully assisted by the Order of the Society of Jesus.

By the end of the century all this was gone. The House of Hapsburg had made the empire an adjunct of its Austrian dominions, while the other German princes, large and small, were "sovereign." Indeed, as G. N. Clark has pointed out, "each of the leading members had greater interests and possessions outside [the empire] than inside it." [4] Thus the elector of Brandenburg was king of the rising Prussian state, the elector of Saxony was king of Poland, the elector of Hanover was heir-presumptive to the throne of England. By the terms of the Peace of Utrecht (1713), the Spanish crown had passed from the Hapsburgs to the House of Bourbon, on condition that it never be united with the French crown. By the time Louis XIV, as the *Roi Soleil*, took over the reins in 1661, France herself was clearly a modern, national state, absolute in its sway. If Cardinal Mazarin had dreamed of securing the ancient imperial throne for his king, these dreams were the last gasp of a moribund world of ideas; the Sun King's ambitions were more prosaic. Dead also was the Counter

---

[3] John Lilburn, *Jonah's Cry out of the Whale's Belly* (1647).
[4] G. N. Clark, *The Seventeenth Century* (Oxford, 1950), p. 89.

Reformation, and with it all hope of reuniting Christianity; St. Peter's successors had ceased to be a major factor in Europe's great politics, and Innocent XI (1676–1689) actually embarked on an anti-Jesuit policy late in the century. At the same time in England a long revolutionary struggle had crystallized in modern constitutionalism, a permanent legacy upon which the more moderate elements could all unite. The Glorious Revolution of 1688–1689 finally settled this issue, when the English "people's" right to settle their own constitution was at last vindicated.

The theoretical origins of the political thought of the age are to be found in the notion of "reason of state." Set forth by the Jesuit Giovanni Botero (1540–1617) in the famous book *Della ragione di stato* (1588), the idea captured the imagination of the early baroque age. Among politically interested men everywhere, and especially in Italy, "reason of state," "*raison d'Etat*," or "*ragione di stato*" was the great subject of discussion and writing. The shift from ethics to politics, or rather the blending of the two through the skillful rationalization of means, illustrated the way in which reason was, in this literature, reinterpreted as meaning the rational means for the accomplishment of ends. Characteristic of this entire literature, and completely in harmony with its origins in the Jesuit Order, was the fact that a distinction was being drawn between a good and a bad reason of state, depending upon the ends to which it was put. The scorn of Machiavelli's frankly pagan and blandly pragmatic mind would have been provoked by this distinction, but to the new baroque minds it was as natural as the curves with which their artists dissolved the stately harmony of Renaissance forms. Hence they argued, "The reason of state is a necessary violation of the common law for the end of public utility." [5] As can be seen from this definition, the notion of particular necessities occasioned by a state's peculiar interests is linked to this idea of a special means-end rationality directed toward the public utility. In the policies of the great statesmen of the age, arguments about the "necessities" of particular states provided the concrete manifestations of the doctrine of reason of state.

But if one assumed that all thought and action followed a single persistent trend, one's comprehension of the problem would be most inadequate. The illustrious names of Grotius, Richelieu, Hobbes, Cromwell, Spinoza, Gustavus Adolphus, and the great elector of Brandenburg all represent the dominant and victorious trend—victorious, that is, in 1660. But there were other men who struggled to resist, in 1610 and for many years thereafter, and these too had their champions in speech and writing. Most important among these opposing groups was the one which endeavored to uphold the cause of the representative estates, and whose arguments ranged all the way from apologies for feudal reaction to the projection of democratic dreams. These forces were not uniformly unsuccessful, as is illustrated by regions in which they did not succumb to the rising absolutism, notably Poland, Sweden, and England.

To the modern mind the word "state" has become so all-embracing in its connotations, so thoroughly permeated with the ideas of sovereignty and independence, that it is difficult to recapture the thought and feeling of an age in

[5] Pietro A. Canonhiero, *Dell'introduzione alla politica, all ragione di stato* . . . (1614).

which the employment of the word to signify unity was a startling, novel concept. It had always been the plural "estates," prior to the seventeenth century, and the English language obscures the connection, which in French is still patent, between *l'Etat* and *les états*. In its typical form the system of *états* was a joint or mixed government by a prince, himself considered an estate, and all the other estates. The division of competence, because it was not very clearly defined, gave the advantage to prince or estates according to circumstances. There was a tendency from the very beginning to consider estates the representatives of the whole community, despite the fact that they appeared to be little more than a collection of various interests, and despite the fact that this view expressed hope more than reality. The significant contrast of this with later conditions, however, lies in the fact that the early estates were looked upon as apart and separate from the lord or prince. Hence, the dualistic nature of the system was expressed when government was said to be *with*, not *by*, estates. Although often overlapping and ill defined, the sphere of competence of both princes and estates was nevertheless thought of as distinct and settled in terms of an agreement. Often called *tractatus* or treaty, this agreement thus expressed the fact that the two authorities were looked upon as distinct entities.

From the multitude of estates which had characterized the mediaeval constitutional order, gradually there emerged the unitary, all-embracing state. Traditionally there had been the several estates: the king, the nobility, the clergy, and the commons united in parliament—to illustrate by the English example. The fundamental outline is not altered by numerous variations in detail; even the rich complexity of the estates of the Holy Roman Empire in central Europe followed the general pattern, but with the added factor of geographical divisions. Local estates had been gaining ground in many territories during the second half of the sixteenth century, and, as we shall see, the fatal cataclysm of the Thirty Years' War (1618–1648) originated in a conflict between the estates of Bohemia and their prince. A disintegration of the mediaeval order is clearly revealed in developments in the seventeenth century, a disintegration characterized by an irreconcilable dualism which, in England, manifested itself in the novel idea that parliament was a thing separate and apart from the king. Although the estates' assemblies occupied different positions in different places, almost all of them operated under a system of government rather similar to that of England. In Italy, to be sure, there were no estates. In Spain, during the sixteenth century, the Cortes had been crushed in Castile, if not in Aragon, while in France, at the beginning of the seventeenth century, the estates were on the point of vanishing, the last assembly being held in 1614. But elsewhere they were holding their own or even challenging the crown in the impending struggle for supremacy.

It is only natural that this system, controversial in its day, should have elicited conflicting interpretations. There are two schools of thought: one has taken the Thirty Years' War as the historical event which destroyed the estates; the other has insisted that the estates were doomed anyway once they had been reduced to the status of dependent corporations by the idea of sovereignty, of monarchical or royal supremacy. In any case, there can be no doubt that once the Reformation had destroyed the unifying potentialities of mediaeval Christianity, the dualistic constitutionalism of a "government with estates" faced issues that were apt to render the collaboration of the divided powers precarious. The struggle for supremacy became more intense as the religious issues injected themselves. "Your . . . Politicians seem unto me rather to have invented some new ammunition, or Gunpowder, in their King and Parliament . . . than Government," wrote the English political theorist James Harrington (1611–1677) shortly after the conclusion of the Thirty Years' War. "For what is become of the Princes (a kind of people) in *Germany?* blown up. Where are the Estates, or the Power of the People, in *France?* blown up. Where is that of the people in *Aragon*, and the rest of the *Spanish* kingdoms? blown up. On the other side, where is the King of *Spain's* power in Holland? blown up. Where is that of the *Austrian* princes in *Switz?* blown up." [6]

That is the setting within which the modern state emerged during the first half of the seventeenth century. During this period estates, except in England, proved to be not only inefficient but actually a hindrance to the effective prosecution of war. So, wherever possible, the princes sought to discard their assemblies altogether. In short, the conflict implied in the dualism between princes and estates was brought to a head in the period of the Thirty Years' War. The system was the heritage of an age united through a common faith. Mediaeval constitutionalism was built upon a division of power between prince and estates, and as such it had rested upon a unity of faith which was now gone. Everywhere the claimants for a "true Christian religion" were ripping wide open the older constitu-

[6] *The Political Writings of James Harrington*, ed. by C. Blitzer (New York, 1955), p. 143.

tional order as they entrenched themselves in the estates' assemblies. Everywhere the conflict between princes and estates was also a conflict between Catholic and Protestant, between Calvinist, Lutheran, and Nonconformist. It is a curious fact that in some ways the most extraordinary spokesman of the political implications of this conflict was to be King James I of England (1566–1625). He, more than anyone else, personified the divine right of kings theoretically claimed by the emergent state: "The State of Monarchie is the supremest thing upon earth," he declared to his first parliament in 1609. "Kings are justly called Gods, for that they exercise a manner or resemblance of Divine power upon earth." [7]

Although James's assertion of absolute monarchical power was still radical at the beginning of the seventeenth century, the grounds on which he made his claims were obsolete by the time Thomas Hobbes's *Leviathan* appeared in 1651. European political thought had been largely secularized during the intervening years. The true significance of Hobbes lies in his attempt to construct an authoritarian system without Biblical underpinnings, rather than in his rational justification of despotism. One finds the same secularizing trend in the camp of the constitutionalists: between 1603 and 1690—from Johannes Althusius (1563–1638), the theorist of government with estates, to John Locke (1632–1704), the philosopher of the Glorious Revolution [8]—con-

[7] *Political Works of James I*, ed. by C. H. McIlwain (Cambridge, Mass., 1918), p. 307.

[8] Peter Laslett has recently shown, though, that the celebrated essay was not written to "justify" the Revolution. It was actually written about eight years *before* the Revolution. See his "The English Revolution and Locke's 'Two Treatises on Government,'" *Cambridge Historical Journal*, XII (1956), 40–55.

stitutionalism became secularized. The central political idea
of these two writers was sovereignty of the people acting
through popularly elected representatives, but whereas
Althusius was much concerned with the Biblical evidence
offered in support of this tenet, Locke relied almost exclusively upon general philosophical argumentation.

Two other ideas besides the central one of "state" were
also fundamental to the newly secularized political thought
of the seventeenth century. One was the concept of natural
law as a superior norm, necessary precisely because the
state and its magistrates were increasingly being accepted
as the ultimate arbiters of human, man-made law. The
other was the concept of "sovereignty" with its attendant
problems of who was "sovereign" and what "sovereignty"
included. The prevalent mediaeval view had been that law
was fixed and, if not immutable, at least changing slowly
and almost imperceptibly. Statutory enactments were usually seen as "interpreting," or making manifest, a law
which was believed to be already there. The new scientific
impetus to discover the regularities according to which the
universe functions contributed directly to the campaign to
discover laws of nature. Hence every political theorist in
this period, absolutist and constitutionalist alike, undertook
to prove that his contentions were logical deductions from
the law of nature. What was this law of nature? The age
was none too sure about its substance. Opinion vacillated
between the older classical concept that the laws of nature
were a collection of just norms, and the new notion that
the laws of nature described the regular course of nature.
The former are exemplified by rules of conduct like the
famous triad of the Roman law, "To live rightly, to hurt
no one, to give everyone his own," while the scientific laws

of nature seemed most awe-inspiring when regulating the motion of heavenly bodies. If scientific laws of nature were being discovered by observation and experiment, just norms had been learned by study of the Bible and by reason. The political thought of the period was inclined to have recourse to both methods; indeed, for many thinkers the fact that God, the lawgiver of the universe, was the author of both sets of regulations obscured, if it did not obliterate, the difference.

The Dutch Calvinist Johannes Althusius, whose *Politica* appeared in 1603, held that the laws of nature were identical with the Ten Commandments, implemented by the Christian doctrine of love. Yet Althusius also undertook to show that commonwealths had been operated in accordance with these natural laws and that, in fact, when they had not they had come to grief. The sanction for the norm therefore was the threat of failure and destruction; the norm was rooted in the facts of nature. Hugo Grotius (1583–1645), on the other hand, attempted to found the law of nature upon human reason and reason alone; reason, he held, could be comprehended without any theological doctrine. Thus war, which during the religious conflicts had gradually deteriorated into the most barbarous slaughter, was once more made subject to certain general rules, obligatory upon Catholic, Protestant, and Mohammedan alike. The absolutist Thomas Hobbes (1588–1679) also agreed that the ruler is bound to observe the laws of nature; nor were Hobbesian laws so very different from those of Althusius or Grotius. But two things were attempted by Hobbes which constitute radical departures: on the one hand, he tried to demonstrate the independent existence of these rules of natural law, and, somewhat contradictorily, he also made them dependent upon the sovereign's will and enforcement. What he seems to say is this: either these so-called natural laws are true laws of nature, i.e., generalizations based upon observed matters of fact, in which case they will always be enforced, or they are merely normative judgments, in which case they will be enforced only to the extent that the sovereign chooses to put his power behind them. Insofar as natural laws possess the quality of existential laws of nature, Hobbes undertook to derive them from his basic conception of human nature, which was built upon the notion that men's actions are determined by passions restrained by the fear of violent death. Thus he interpreted the law of nature as a system of rules of prudence, dictated by reason, to be sure, but not the higher reason founded on faith. The Copernican revolution of the view of the law of nature which Hobbes had begun was completed by Baruch Spinoza (1632–1677), the Dutch Jew. Whereas Hobbes's system, though diluted through utilitarian calculations, still recognized a natural law with moral connotations, Spinoza radically asserted the completely naturalistic tenet that might makes right: "The big fish devour the little fish by natural right." Written about 1660, this debonair sentence states with sweeping skepticism the actual practice of politics as pursued by Richelieu, Mazarin, the Hapsburgs, and the Hohenzollerns. These ideas found striking theoretical expression in the work of Samuel Pufendorf (1632–1694). The older, normative conception of natural law, on the other hand, continued to find able supporters throughout the seventeenth century. The most outstanding of these was John Locke (1632–1704), who presented a modernized version of the traditional Christian view: "The state of nature has a law of nature to govern it, which obliges every one; and reason, which is that law, teaches all mankind . . . that, being all equal and independent, no one ought to harm another in his life, health, liberty, or possessions." [9] Whereas Hobbes's "ought" was simply a prudential rule, Locke's was clearly a moral norm.

It is fascinating to see how these ideas on natural law, common yet conflicting, were reflected in a similar body of thought on sovereignty and state absolutism. For, like Hobbes and Spinoza, Althusius and Grotius were convinced that in any commonwealth worthy of the name there must be a sovereign authority, a supreme ruler. Here the preoccupation with law intruded itself once more. For the sovereign ruler must give laws to the state as God had given the laws to the cosmos. In other words, order, presupposing laws, cannot prevail where there is no lawgiving organ or body. There seems never to have been any dissent, either absolutist or constitutionalist, from the tenet that the most important function in the state is the legislative function. Yet, the establishment of central administration was undoubtedly the most striking institutional development of the period. The most important function of these administrative staffs, in the opinion of seventeenth-century minds, was to make the law "conducive to a well-ordered polity." It is highly significant that even John Locke never dreamed of claiming this legislative function for "the legislature" alone. On the contrary, its very importance required the full participation of the king and his administra-

[9] John Locke, *Second Treatise of Civil Government*, ed. by J. W. Gough (Oxford, 1948), ch. ii, p. 5.

tive staff. Thus, whether exercised by monarch or popular representatives or both, sovereignty was vindicated as the law-making authority and was admitted to be bound by natural law.

How could such awful, godlike power of giving laws to men ever be acquired legitimately? This portentous question, which produced the greatest amount of controversy in the seventeenth century, was characteristically answered by the argument that there must be a law according to which sovereign power is established—a law which the seventeenth century found in contract. The idea of contract, intimately linked with the life and work of the trading middle classes as it was, quite naturally developed into a potent idea in the circles in which political thought was being secularized throughout this age. Indeed, its usefulness is symbolized by the fact that, like the idea of natural law, it became a weapon in the hands of both absolutists and constitutionalists. Thomas Hobbes was the philosopher of power par excellence. More than any other man he penetrated to the very core of the enthusiasm of his age and rationalized it in sweeping, overwhelming generalizations. His was the most secular view of the omnipotent state as a system by which the universe of human life was ordered. Humanist and scholar rather than man of affairs, Hobbes was convinced throughout his life that absolute monarchy was the best form of government, and he showed that the contractual argument could be molded into a tool for the support of this very absolutism. In his *Leviathan*, Hobbes pictures man living in a "state of nature," characterized by the "war of every man, against every man":

In such condition, there is no place for industry; because the fruit thereof is uncertain: and consequently no culture of the earth; no navigation, nor use of the commodities that may be imported by sea; no commodious building; . . . no arts; no letters; no society; and which is worst of all, continual fear, and danger of violent death; and the life of man, solitary, poor, nasty, brutish and short.[10]

Faced with the horrors of this anarchy, Hobbes argues, individuals contracted among themselves to submit altogether to an absolute sovereign. Similarly, Hugo Grotius urged that the people could transfer, and evidently often had transferred, the sovereign power by contract, explicit, tacit, or implied. The more common use of the contract argument, however, was as a buttress for limited, or constitutional, government. Perhaps the most notable example of this school of thought is John Locke's *Second Treatise of Civil Government* (1690):

Whosoever, therefore, out of a state of nature unite into a community must be understood to give up all the power necessary to the ends for which they unite into society to the majority of the community. . . . And this is done by barely agreeing to unite into one political society, which is all the compact that is, or needs be, between individuals that enter into or make up a commonwealth. And thus that which begins and actually constitutes any political society is nothing but the consent of any number of freemen capable of a majority to unite and incorporate into such a society. And this is that, and that only, which did or could give beginning to any lawful government in the world.[11]

---

[10] Hobbes, *op. cit.*, pt. I, ch. xiii, p. 82.
[11] Locke, *op. cit.*, ch. viii, pp. 49–50.

In tone, in content, and even in style, the contrast between these two passages may serve as a measure of the rapid development of political thought during the half century that separates them.

Conclusion

The underlying common core of the seventeenth century —the new sense of power which characterized it—is revealed in our rapid sketch of the variegated patterns of political and economic thought and institutions. Who is to say whether the modern state emerged in this period because some of its most striking representatives were filled with this sense of power, or whether they were filled with this sense of power because the modern state emerged? It is clear in any case that the two developments were closely linked and that they molded the fundamental outlook and feeling of man in the seventeenth century, his "climate of opinion," to use the phrase invented by the English *savant* Joseph Glanvill (1636–1680). From this "climate of opinion" came the style that has come to be known as baroque —the style in which Renaissance elements, consisting of revived forms of classical antiquity, were molded into a new and specifically western form. Before we can see the extraordinary stage upon which were enacted the gigantic dramas of the Thirty Years' War, the building of modern absolutism by Richelieu, and the English revolution, we must explore more fully the essential characteristics of this new style in its varied manifestations in literature, art, and thought. Such a stage western civilization had not seen before, nor has it since.

CHAPTER II

The Baroque

THE new sense of power which characterized every form of human expression and creativity in the seventeenth century is nowhere more apparent than in the artistic style of the age—the baroque. And, indeed, it could hardly be otherwise, for men express through their works of art, their creations of beauty, what they have experienced and have thought to be true. Style is a mysterious quality, true only if spontaneous and spontaneous only if a projection of genuine feeling and true experience. In this sense, there can be no doubt that the baroque was a true style, and surely no other, neither Gothic nor Renaissance, has left so vast and dominant an imprint upon the European scene.

In time, the baroque extended roughly from the middle of the sixteenth century to the middle of the eighteenth, reaching its height about 1660. Like all styles, it had no uniform set of traits, but can be thought of as the product of tension between a series of extremes operating within a common field of ideas and feelings. This common field of feeling was focused on movement, intensity, tension, and force. In the palace and the opera, two creations which are the result of harmonious blending of many art forms, baroque art found its richest fulfillment. Palace and opera are manifold units. Baroque architecture produced the richly ornamented façade, the sweep of magnificent staircases, the ornamental garden as a setting of the palace and a foreground of a distant view. Baroque painting reveled in the effects of light and shadow, employed the intermediate shades of many-hued grays, browns, and greens, and, through the portrayal of landscape and of the human face, explored the subtleties of individuality in nature. Theater and drama, especially the form of the heroic tragedy, seemed peculiarly adapted to the baroque spirit in the field of letters; but the extravagant comedy, fairy tale, knightly novel, and ornate lyrics were also characteristic baroque creations. In all forms, baroque developed the art of effective characterization, both of individuals and of types, but particularly the latter.[1] First Spain and then France took the lead. Finally, in baroque music the expressive depicting of emotional states and sentiments reached a high level, first in the solo parts of opera and oratorio, soon afterward in the varying combinations of stringed instruments, and finally in gigantic combinations of human voices and instrumental music, both in the oratorio and in the opera.

Where did this new style come from? A profound revolution of the spirit is clearly manifest in it since it molded all spheres of life and art. It has been argued that the Counter Reformation—the Catholic Reformation of the late sixteenth century—was the embodiment of this revolution. The argument can scarcely be maintained in this simple form of describing baroque art as the direct expres-

---

[1] Recently, Jean Rousset has argued that disguise is very important to baroque style, and he has interpreted Don Juan in this context. See *Diogenes*, XIV (1956), 1–16.

sion of the spirit of the Counter Reformation. The extreme religiosity of the early Catholic reformers (notably Pope Pius V, 1565–1572), the fact that the Counter Reformation was nearly dead in the period when the baroque culminated, and the fact that many of the finest flowers of the baroque style were the creation of Protestant people, all clearly demonstrate the inadequacy of this explanation. In part, however, the baroque style is animated by ideas and feelings which the Reformation and Counter Reformation had ushered in. New forms of political thought gave expression to the violent clash of religion and politics, of church and state; the amoral paganism of Renaissance Italy gave way to tortuous rationalizing, to a search for moral "justification" for doing what was necessary. Baroque, as contrasted with the debonair worldliness of the Renaissance, was tormented by doubts and shot through with conflicts and tension. The baroque was an age torn between extremes, an age in which a gross sensuality alternating with pangs of conscience, rather than a happy and unreflective pleasure of the senses, became the dominant note. While the philosophical and scholarly inquiries of Humanism led to skepticism and scientific discovery, the worldliness of the Renaissance turned to coarse materialism and carnal debauch. On the other hand, otherworldly beliefs were intensified by the religious protest against Renaissance and Humanism which Reformation and Counter Reformation share. A fierce moral fanaticism which often culminated in arid dogmatism and intolerant persecution, in superstition and violence, was strengthened by the revival of religion. The Counter Reformation, since it undoubtedly contributed its share to the ideas and feelings which animated the baroque artist, constituted an essential ingredient of these conflicting attitudes.

Another school has held that the dominant impulse for the baroque style originated in the life of the monarchical courts under absolutism. The basis for this view is the well-known patronage which the princes of seventeenth century Europe bestowed upon the art of the time. Without doubt some of the most characteristic creations of the baroque style were courtly, such as the sumptuous palace, set within a vast complex of artificially created parks and gardens, or the opera, which made its first appearance as part of lavish court festivals. Yet therefore to make baroque *the* art of monarchial absolutism, to link the feelings of baroque solely to the particular political structure of absolutist monarchy is going too far. Many of the most beautiful edifices of the baroque period were ecclesiastical—churches, cloisters, abbeys—and this is not all. There were the rich bourgeois, not only in these absolute monarchies but also in England, Holland, Venice, and elsewhere, who bought the canvases of painters, built beautiful town houses, and freely supported the new musical forms of opera, oratorio, and symphony. Such artists as Rembrandt van Rijn (1606–1669), Nicolas Poussin (1594–1665), and Claude Lorrain (1600–1682) were indifferent, if not actually hostile, to court life. The plays and oratorios of stage and church, although fostered by the princes, were not the exclusive privilege of the few, but rather were the common possession of all; perhaps they most significantly expressed the spirit of the age.

Baroque sought to give literary and artistic expression to an age which was intoxicated with the power of man; perhaps in some ways its fascination with the impossible is thus explained. At the height of the baroque, architects, sculptors, painters, poets, and musicians strove to accomplish the impossible in *all* directions. Hence radical naturalism vied with extreme formalism, materialism vied with spiritualism, the most terrifying realism with the most precious illusionism. Metaphysical poetry sought to probe into ultimate mysteries, while voluptuous and lascivious erotic poetry violated all canons of good taste. Excited beyond measure by the potentialities of man, such an age was able to establish the foundations of modern science through some of its representatives, while through others it persecuted old women as witches; for both activities presume an exaggerated belief in the power of man to think and to act as he confronts with heightened powers a mysterious, exciting world. God orders the universe by his limitless will; Satan by a comparable effort seeks to disturb this order. The fascination which the figure of Satan had for John Milton (1608–1674) was born of admiration for the kind of strength that will challenge rather than be subordinated. The statesmen of this age made a cult of power and of its adornments: the vast spectacle, the impenetrable intrigue, the gruesome murder. Such a sense of power calls for a capacity in the artist to portray, and to dramatize, tension; that is the quintessence of baroque.

The extraordinary artistic productivity of the period 1610–1713, itself an indication of the vitality of the baroque age, makes impossible even a bare enumeration of its outstanding creations. Having discussed the general qualities of the baroque style, we must now be content simply to illustrate its manifestations in the various branches of the arts, showing how the same essential spirit informs the work of architect and painter, playwright and sculptor, musician and poet.

Personal Behavior

Before coming to the arts, however, it will perhaps be useful to say a few words about the baroque element in personal behavior during the seventeenth century. Indeed, it may be argued that one of the most revealing aspects of the baroque age was the very fact that at this time personal behavior became, in a very real sense, one of the arts. Throughout Europe, men of high estate thought of themselves as living upon a stage, and their every action was calculated to produce a desired effect. There are peculiarities of personal behavior by which an age or nation is seen, as it were, "naked to the watchful eye," and the wig is probably the most revealing symbol of the baroque. Legend attributes its origin to Louis XIII, who, it is said, wished to hide his baldness, but in fact it vividly expressed that desire to push things to the extreme and to cultivate the theatrical exaggeration of reality. Hair became longer, beards more flowing and dramatic in the first generation of the century, but as the century progressed, beards and mustaches became smaller and eventually vanished, for they hide the face instead of setting it off as does a wig.

Costumes were very stately and elaborate, except where startling simplifications resulted from strong moral convictions; a highly dramatic effect was achieved by the Puritans and the Jansenist fellowship of Port Royal [2] in their monklike uniformity, as by individuals like Richelieu's colleague Father Joseph, the "Gray Eminence." Ladies' fashions, often bordering on disguise, were similarly elaborate. The

[2] See below, Chapter III.

passion of the age for dressing up in weird attire led even the exalted, such as the king of Spain, to indulge in occasional masques.

The sense of "face" was as highly developed as in the Orient, and men went to great lengths to avenge any infringement of their honor. Honor became the most sought-after sign of power, and the endless quarreling and dueling took such a toll of the aristocracy in France (and other countries) that the government felt compelled to take vigorous measures to combat it. Corneille's dramas [3] were preoccupied with the portrayal of clashes of honor, and the stage of Spain, England, and Germany was dominated by the same theme.

At the same time, gross sensuality engulfed both high and low. The excesses in eating and drinking were a universal habit, although probably most extreme at the German courts; in Italy and France they took the subtler forms of elaborate gourmanderie. These lusts of the palate were associated with violent sexual debauchery, both male and female, and there was a contrasting fanatical enthusiasm for chastity, which may be considered a perverted form of sexuality. The cloisters of Spain and France, Port Royal and other similar circles, together with the notorious puritanical extremists, were as characteristic of the age as the libidinous and licentious court circles of Britain, France, and Spain, Italy and Germany. The common folk gloried in the exhibitionism of sexual swagger as much as the aristocracy. Yet, contrasted with the Renaissance and later periods, there was a displayful enthusiasm for the passions as such, and an unprecedented sense of the drama inherent in the struggle

[3] See below, p. 30.

between these passions and the rational mind, a struggle in which their role was heightened by clerical efforts to control them.

The baroque view of man was closely linked to these aspects of personal behavior. Emphasis was on action, constant combat, personal success, and the resultant heightening of the sense of self. The ceremonial of social contact expressed the pervading and intense sense of personal dignity and gravity. Baroque man believed that the passions were central to man's essence and stressed having, rather than being, something. Descartes, Hobbes, Pascal, Spinoza [4] all philosophized in terms of the passions and their great power over human destiny, seeking to explore and understand them; hence the beginning of psychology in their generation. At the same time man, struggling passionately and willfully to master his fate, was seen as fate's helpless victim. Highly symbolic of the baroque were the meteoric rise and the cataclysmic fall of favorites, conquering heroes and royal concubines. It is almost as if the baroque age had insisted that the most striking exhibition of man's never-ending quest for power was to find a final consummation in violent death or, at the least, banishment, exile, oblivion.

Literature

The figure of Satan in Milton's *Paradise Lost* (1667) was perhaps as striking a portrayal of baroque man as the age created:

> . . . aspiring
> To set himself in Glory above his Peers,
> He trusted to have equalled the most High,

[4] See below, Chapter III.

If he oppos'd; and with ambitious aim
Against the Throne and Monarchy of God,
Rais'd impious War in Heav'n, and Battel proud,
With vain attempt.[5]

Yet, one must try to imagine Milton together with Pierre Corneille (1606–1684) and Pedro Calderón de la Barca (1600–1681), Joost van den Vondel (1587–1679) and Molière (1622–1673), John Dryden (1631–1700), Jean Baptiste Racine (1639–1699), and Hans von Grimmelshausen (1620–1676), to appreciate the fullness of his baroque stature. Not only was *Paradise Lost* the Protestant response to the challenge of the Italian *dramma di musica,* but it also sounded the counterpoint to the entire dramatic poetry of the Renaissance, especially that of Shakespeare and Spencer. Renaissance elements were present in the work of these baroque writers to some extent, as they were in all baroque forms: these forms were an attempt to combine the formal perfection of the preceding age with the sense of the working of supernatural powers within and beyond man. Deeply metaphysical, the baroque poets and writers strained their powers of formal art to the utmost in order to capture the sense of these dynamic forces—thus reveling in movement, in colorful and violent contrasts, in the aggregation of descriptive adjectives and exclamatory nouns. These dramas, epics, and great chorales reveal a tremendous power of imagination at work. True children of the century of rational intelligence, these writers celebrated self-esteem and gravity, pomp and heroic pathos, as expressive of secular and religious passions. Tension and struggle were everywhere. Poets and writers carried both sober rational-

[5] *Paradise Lost,* in *The Works of John Milton,* (New York, 1931), vol. II, bk. 1, ll. 38–44.

ism and deeply felt emotionalism to extremes of formal self-expression. Their language is highly ornate, and they maintained rigorous forms at the cost of an artificiality which is often highly irritating to modern ears. Strange flowers are produced by the great passions which pulsate beneath this formal structure, flowers which obscure the view like ice-ferns on the window in deep winter. Milton's description of the procession of evil spirits leagued with Satan abounds in such baroque word-painting.[6] Tortuous similes as well as classical allusions were beloved by all these writers. But their most urgent concern was the portrayal of human passions, which they saw as proliferations of supernatural powers rather than as strictly human characteristics familiar to the Renaissance and to Humanism.

Spain in the first half of the seventeenth century experienced the baroque most intensely as the genuine form of its literary genius; indeed, it may be said that in the baroque Spain found her true form and fulfillment. Leaving aside the immortal Cervantes (1547–1616), whose *Don Quixote* (1605 and 1615) belongs "not to an age, but to all time," one is confronted with the towering figures of Tirso de Molina (1571–1648), the priest who wrote impudent comedies and devout sacred plays of deep wisdom; Góngora y Argote (1561–1627), the subtle lyricist; Lope de Vega (1562–1635), the creator of nearly a thousand dramas, epics, lyrics, and sacred plays; and finally Calderón de la Barca (1600–1681), the great dramatist—they constitute the flowering of the Spanish genius in literature. The dynamic tensions of the baroque, the inherent antagonism between its idealistic, ardent spirituality and its earthy, passionate sensuality, find a deep response in Spain's native

[6] *Ibid.*, bk. I, ll. 331–571.

inclinations. Hand in hand with its exaggerated formalism and the search for subtle and complex ornamentation go poignant naturalism and erotic intensity.

In literature, as in so many other fields, the latter part of the century was dominated by the influence of France; this was truly the age of Louis XIV. Characteristically, it was in the reign of Louis—prototype of absolute monarchy—that the canons of literary taste came to be most rigidly defined and stylistic uniformity most strictly enforced. The French preference for precision and refinement of style, the so-called "preciousness," led finally to *L'Art poétique* (1674) of Nicolas Boileau, in which acceptable modes of literary expression were codified; so pervasive was this French influence that the English poet John Dryden literally copied many of Boileau's *dicta* in his critical writings. As in Spain, so in France the baroque found its most fitting literary expression in the drama; but the French genius brought to the baroque world-picture some specifically French sentiments which resulted in greater stress upon gravity and severity of form than in Spain. Corneille particularly was a true baroque dramatist in the ornate quality of his language, the abstract and type-formed character of his figures, and his climactic enhancement of formalized conflict situations. Under the influence of the Cartesian passion for "clear and distinct ideas," [7] and with the active support of the court, this formal element increased in importance throughout the century, as the drama became at the same time more stylized and more analytical. It is perhaps most apparent in the great comedies of Molière: *Le Tartuffe* (1664), *Le Bourgeois Gentilhomme* (1670), *Le Malade imaginaire* (1673), and some thirty

[7] See below, Chapter III.

others in which society was skillfully dissected and its follies laid bare with devastating wit. What Molière had done for the less exalted aspects of human nature, Jean Racine, in his great tragedies, and particularly in his *Phèdre* (1677), did for passion. The analytical clarity and the rigid adherence to form which characterizes them both is as baroque as the clipped hedges of Versailles.

Even so brief a survey of the literature of the seventeenth century would be incomplete without some mention of developments outside Spain and France. In Holland the century produced that country's greatest dramatist, Joost van den Vondel; it has been said that "Vondel, in the often clumsy, but always aspiring majesty of his elevated, solemn language is the perfect baroque poet." [8] Very different in spirit and influence was the *Simplicissimus* (1669) of the German Grimmelshausen, a striking novel of adventure depicting the horrors of life during the Thirty Years' War. Finally, in England, the age produced both the religious allegory of John Bunyan's *The Pilgrim's Progress* (1678), an expression of the mystical strain which was so central to the baroque, and the poems of John Dryden, the rationalist par excellence.

The only common denominator which enables us to conceive of these literary creations as varied expressions of a common view of man and the world is the omnipresent sense of power in all its forms, spiritual and secular, scientific and political, psychological and technical. Man's startling achievements produced in him a sense of potential might which alternated with a crushing realization of human limitations in the face of an infinite world created by

[8] J. Huizinga, *Holländische Kultur des Siebzehnten Jahrhunderts* (Jena, 1933), p. 43.

a remote and all-powerful being who transcended all human comprehension. Poets of true grandeur found in the inherent drama of such a view a magnificent setting for their works. It is the glory of the baroque age that everywhere men rose to this unique challenge; they all spoke the language of an age in which man's dignity was his most prized possession, with which he faced the powers of this earth and those of the beyond.

Architecture, Sculpture, and Painting

The term "baroque" was originally coined to describe the architectural style that dominated the European scene from the late sixteenth century to the early eighteenth. As is so often the case with such stylistic periods, the lines that delimit the beginning and the end of baroque architecture are unclear: the late work of Michelangelo (d. 1564) has been considered the beginning of the baroque, while the kinship between baroque style and rococo is so great that the rococo of the early eighteenth century has aptly been called no more than a lighter and more gracious form of the baroque. One may say, however, that the earliest clearly baroque building is the church of Il Gesù, built by the Jesuits in Rome between 1568 and 1584; furthermore, with the exception of Germany and eastern Europe, where the development came somewhat later, the period between 1630 and 1690 was the age of the so-called "high baroque," the supreme fulfillment of the style.

Closely associated with the turn toward the high baroque was the career of Giovanni Lorenzo Bernini (1598–1680), the greatest figure of the age in both architecture and sculpture, two arts which at this time enter into so intimate a relationship that the one is inconceivable without the other.

Among Bernini's most impressive creations are the great colonnaded plaza of St. Peter's, the tombs of popes Urban VIII and Alexander VII, the superb bust of Louis XIV and the St. Theresa altar piece in the church of Santa Maria della Vittoria in Rome. In his works, the tension, the movement, the dynamic challenge that characterize baroque architecture and sculpture found their supreme embodiment.

From its birthplace in Italy, baroque architecture spread rapidly throughout Europe during the century, first north to France and England, then east to Germany and the Slavic world. Today, no great European city is imaginable without the rich creations of baroque architecture and sculpture: the rhythmic façades, the sweeping staircases, the flowing lines, the broad curves, and the skillful use of light and shadow to unify the whole. Indeed, so rich was this baroque harvest that only a few particularly notable examples can be mentioned here. In France, where baroque architecture, like baroque literature, was restrained by a regard for classic forms, the great palace of Versailles, with its elaborately ordered plan and formalized setting, served as a fitting expression of the disciplined court of the *Roi Soleil*. The famous eastern façade of the Louvre, despite the fact that the design of Claude Perrault was chosen over that submitted by Bernini, stands as another monument of the baroque, while Jules Hardouin-Mansart's church of Les Invalides embodies perfectly the French compromise between classical and baroque forms—a compromise which, in a larger sense, may be called typically baroque. In England the baroque was not a popular style. Nevertheless, such an impressive example as St. Paul's Cathedral, rebuilt by Sir Christopher Wren (1632–1723) after the great fire of 1666, still dominates London, while Blenheim Palace, designed by Sir John Vanbrugh (1664–1726), stands as a monument to the duke of Marlborough. To the east, where the lighter rococo influence was dominant around the turn of the century, one must mention the work of Johann Bernard Fischer von Erlach (1656–1723) in Bavaria and Austria, and the superb *Zwinger* (palace) of Matthaus Daniel Poeppelmann (1662–1736) in Dresden.

In the painting of the baroque period, the same general tendencies which molded architecture and sculpture were, of course, at work. But here the baroque also developed certain other formal elements. Among the outstanding traits of the new and vital style were the extensive use of tonal gradation rather than clear colors, combined with the gradual elimination of distinct outlines and the merging of objects into the surrounding background; chiaroscuro (the contrast of light and shade); and finally the employment of large quantities of pigment and the consequent visibility of brush strokes.

All the great nations of Europe, with the exception of England and Germany, produced magnificent painters in the period of the high baroque. In the early seventeenth century we find the Italians in the lead with Guido Reni (1575–1642) and with the more important Pietro da Cortona (1596–1669). Farther north, the brilliant work of Peter Paul Rubens (1577–1640) with its rich sensuality and color unquestionably dominated the first phase of the high baroque. Rubens, whose influence throughout Europe was tremendous, found perhaps his greatest follower in the more subtle and delicate portraitist Anthony Van Dyck (1599–1641), the court painter of Charles I of England. But if

Van Dyck was a pupil of Rubens, his true kinship was with the even greater Rodríguez de Silva y Velázquez (1599–1660), the court painter of Philip IV of Spain, in whose works a Renaissance clarity is still apparent, as it is in those of his countryman Bartolomé Esteban Murillo (1617–1682). In painting, as in the other arts, one finds the characteristically classical French form of baroque: the artificial, orderly heroic landscapes of Poussin form a perfect counterpart to the dramas of Corneille, while the quietly lyric paintings of Lorrain give superb expression to the baroque sense of unity. The basic polarity of the age is nowhere better illustrated than in the contrast between the work of a great court painter such as Le Brun, the decorator of Versailles, and the work of the greatest Dutch baroque, rooted in the life and feeling of the common folk, the burgher and peasant of the Dutch lowlands, especially as exemplified in Frans Hals (1580–1666) and Rembrandt van Rijn. Among the incredible welter of brilliant talent that illuminated western painting, these two were perhaps the most striking baroque figures, although such men as Jacob Van Ruisdael (1628–1682) and Jan Vermeer (1632–1675) certainly have great claims upon our recognition. Perhaps Frans Hals was the most extreme representative of that lust for life and nature which the age offered. In the work of Rembrandt, however, baroque painting rose to universal significance and appeal. Rembrandt's originality, in its final and perhaps ultimate combination, was revealed in "The Return of the Prodigal Son" (1668–1669); his intense religiosity was here given final form, the inner light of Protestant faith animating not only the painter, but the abject figure of the son, the face of the father, forgiving and sorrowful, and the reverent attitude of the onlookers wrapped in darkness. Here the ultimate in the spirit of baroque feeling was achieved.

Music

In considering the development of music during the seventeenth century, one must take particular care to avoid treating the creations of this period as little more than preparations for the masterpieces of the two supreme baroque composers, Johann Sebastian Bach (1685–1750) and George Frederick Handel (1685–1759). As one becomes familiar with the compositions of men such as Claudio Monteverdi (1567–1643) and Girolamo Frescobaldi (1583–1643), Henry Purcell (1659–1695) and Heinrich Schütz (1585–1672), it is apparent that, quite apart from their historical role, these men deserve a place among the great creative artists of the age; they represent the unfolding of a new style of musical composition in which emotionalism and rationalism, naturalism and formalism, found a dynamic outlet comparable to the creations of baroque architecture and painting, and, indeed, surpassing them.

In music, as in architecture, the development of the baroque style began in Italy, with the creation of an entirely new art form, the *dramma di musica*, or opera. Intimately associated with the so-called "monodic revolution" of the early seventeenth century, which substituted for counterpoint a simpler form of music sung by a single voice with instrumental accompaniment, the baroque opera reached its greatest heights with Monteverdi. Unlike the rather stiff productions of his predecessors, the operas of Monteverdi, notably his *Orfeo* (1607) and *The Coronation of Poppea* (1642), were all conceived in the spirit of unity and power, of deep emotion and stately ritual, in which the baroque gloried. In France, where the opera soon became a fixture of the royal court, Jean Baptiste Lully (1633–1687) wrote a major tragic opera each year from 1673 until his death, establishing a formality in music similar to that of the poetic tragedy. As might be expected, it was at the court of Louis XIV, under Lully, that the first disciplined orchestra was created and orchestral conducting made an exact art. In England, too, under the restored Stuarts, opera dominated the musical scene; Purcell's *Dido and Aeneas* (1689) ranks among the most moving and dramatic works of the century. These new operas may be considered the crowning fulfillment of the life of baroque man, at once stately and playful, enchanted by illusion and yet full of life, reaching out for the infinite in an ecstatic sense of man's power and at the same time full of a sense of cosmic unity and of the passing of time, of the death that seals all life's ambitions and glories. In Germany, in the wake of the disastrous Thirty Years' War, the more somber and spiritual side of the baroque was revealed in the great church music of masters such as Schütz, Paul Gerhardt (1607–1676), and Dietrich Buxtehude (1637–1707). Finally, instrumental music flourished throughout the century, particularly in Italy; the works of Frescobaldi, Arcangelo Corelli (1653–1713), Alessandro Scarlatti (1659–1725) and his son Domenico (1685–1757), and Antonio Vivaldi (1675–1743) were a source of inspiration to Bach and Handel.

Conclusion

The high baroque, with its vast array of wonderful creations in literature, the arts, and music, tempts one to proclaim it the highwater mark of European creative effort.

The sense of limitless power, checked by an overwhelming sense of cosmic relationships, produced a style which startles by its contrasts, yet at the same time exhibits a singular and unique unity. The creators of this style thought that they were continuing and developing the art of the Renaissance, the letters of Humanism, and yet recapturing something of the spirituality of Gothic Christianity. Many of these artists and writers would have been greatly surprised to be called "baroque," since they strove for classic design and perfect beauty. The baroque, like its great predecessor, the Gothic, received its name from critics who did not sympathize with its profound intensity, its sweeping vitality, and its heaven-scaling grandeur.

CHAPTER III

The Power of Mind and Spirit

"BUT you have ordered everything according to measure, number and weight." This line from the Wisdom of Solomon, a favorite quotation in the early seventeenth century, may be called the motto of all scientific effort since that time. But it was characteristic of the seventeenth century that the new passion for the quantitative analysis of all phenomena should express itself by a quotation from the Bible. Efforts to achieve scientific insight were believed to be undertaken "for the greater glory of God," and yet, during the decisive fifty years after 1600, the place of science and religion changed radically. The mathematical and cosmological speculations of Galileo, Kepler, and Descartes laid the foundation for the new world view which with Newton and Leibniz later in the century was well launched on the triumphal career that was to culminate in our time. Characteristically, all three still acknowledged the superior authority of religion, if not of theology. Few writers saw fit to deny the existence of a personal God until Spinoza came to identify God and nature in a pantheistic system that in some respects anticipated the deistic "natural religion" of the next century.

"The Varieties of Religious Experience"

In 1610, roughly two generations after the Council of
Trent, the forces of the Catholic Counter Reformation
were everywhere on the advance. In many countries the
rival factions of Calvinists and Lutherans appeared to be
more concerned with combating each other than with re-
sisting the ever-broadening advance of the Counter Reformation. What had begun in the sixteenth century as a
movement to purify the doctrine and reform the practice
of the Roman Catholic Church had, by the seventeenth
century, divided Christendom into a number of hostile
and apparently irreconcilable confessions. It would, however, be difficult to describe the residual basic disagreements
between Catholics and Protestants, between Lutherans and
Calvinists, that really divided Christendom in 1610. If questions of church government and ecclesiastical organization
played a very important role, so did doctrinal issues, such
as those of the Immaculate Conception, of predestination,
and of the communion, which were hotly debated by intel-
lectuals and simple folk alike, while the more tangible
sources of immediate conflict in family, town, and court
were more often provided by their ethical and political
implications. When the great Grotius published his *De
veritate religionis Christianae* (1627), in which he suggested
that the views of all varieties of Christianity might be rec-
onciled if a common basis of piety were stressed and doctrinal differences minimized, he was immediately acclaimed
by a large number of thoughtful men throughout Europe
who were weary of the endless arguments. But this was
two years before the Edict of Restitution,[1] the highwater

[1] See below, pp. 86–87.

mark of the policy of conversion by force, sought to destroy the secular power of Protestantism in northern Europe. Despite the eventual triumph of something very much like Grotius' ideal of Christian unity, the history of the seventeenth century can only be written in terms of the conflicts—intellectual, military, and political—among dissident branches of Christianity.

On the Catholic side, the most influential and in many ways the most interesting group was the Jesuits. Forcefully led and devotedly concerned with the renewal of the Church of Rome as the universal order, the Society of Jesus had by 1610 achieved a position of extraordinary leadership within the rising tide of Counter Reformation effort. Now chiefly famed for diplomacy and statecraft, the Jesuits in the seventeenth century were far more interesting from a religious standpoint; their strictly political activities were incidental to their great efforts in the fields of education and the arts, especially architecture and the drama. These efforts were doctrinally rooted in the central tenets of the order contained in two writings of the founder Ignatius of Loyola: the *General Examen* and the celebrated *Spiritual Exercises.* The aim of the society as formulated by Loyola was "not only to seek with the aid of the Divine Grace the salvation of one's own soul, but with the aid of the same earnestly to labor for the salvation and perfection of one's neighbor." This concern with each human being gave the order its popular slant and its determination to use every available means to reach the heart and mind of even the lowliest man. Taken together with its devotion to the ideal of a universal church and its insistence upon the personal leadership of Christ, this Jesuit doctrine within the church can usefully be compared to the concept of divine kingship over national communities in the secular realm: they exalted the position of the ruler (pope) in the interest of the mass of followers, while curbing all intermediate powers. As a result, the Jesuits were keenly interested in all the intellectual and artistic currents of sixteenth- and seventeenth-century Europe; not only science, but also humanism and classicism, music and the theater, painting, sculpture, and architecture all became means for their mission of working for "the greater glory of God." Instead of the antithesis between the religious and the secular, between Christian and pagan forms of thought, which had been the characteristic feature of the Renaissance, these opposites were resolved into a new unity, which found expression in the aggressive proselytizing of the new order.

In the course of the seventeenth century, the outlook of the Jesuit order became increasingly worldly, as its members turned more and more to political and commercial activity. Instead of permeating the world with religious enthusiasm, the Jesuits themselves surrendered to the world; they strove to become indispensable to other men and shaped the confessional to this purpose. This description of the Jesuit point of view was expounded and defended by members of the order in a series of works, some of which were even put on the Index. In their defense they relied chiefly upon the conception of sin as a voluntary deviation from divine rule, implying (as their enemies were quick to point out) that man was the more likely to sin the more aware he became of divine rules, while the ignorant or passionate might be considered free of blame. Many Catholics found this doctrine, to say nothing of the practices which it was intended to justify, completely unacceptable. In particular, the movement known as Jansenism, most brilliantly represented by the French Catholic philosopher Blaise Pascal (1623–1662), was violently anti-Jesuit.

The originator of Jansenism was Cornelis Jansen (1585–1638), a Dutch scholar and bishop of Ypres. Jansen's great work, *Augustinus* (published posthumously in 1640), contained a careful digest of the teachings of St. Augustine with emphasis upon the problems confronting the seventeenth century. In this, as in his other books, Jansen urged that religious experience, as contrasted with theological dogma, was the heart of religion; consequently, the "love of God" and faith in Him were more important than any ritual. While Jansen was a scholar, his followers established themselves as a religious movement, with its center at Port Royal, a Cistercian abbey a few miles southwest of Paris. When Pope Innocent X at the behest of the Jesuits and of the French government declared Jansen's work heretical, he opened a dramatic and fateful debate. Blaise Pascal, who at the age of twenty-four had discovered God as He was revealed by the Jansenists, undertook a direct attack on the position of the Jesuits. In his *Provincial Letters* (1656–1657), a series of presumed discussions between Jesuits and Jansenists on a variety of theological subjects, he revealed the startling contrast between the radically ascetic attitude of Jansenist moral perfectionism and the worldly rationalism of the Jesuits as manifested in their defense of such actions as assassination of tyrants and usury (the taking of interest). This most telling incrimination caused an immediate sensation throughout France. In 1660 the convinced authoritarian Louis XIV, as one of his first independent acts, had the Jansenists condemned; the following year all suspects were forced to sign a solemn renunciation. Yet the Jesuits in France never fully recovered from the shattering logic of Pascal's attack; four generations later their order was actually suppressed.

Raging during the very years when the sectarians of the "inner light" battled for the freedom of religious conscience in Protestant England,[2] the Jansenist controversy may be summed up in Pascal's proposition that the church persuades by reason and that "the popes may be surprised." But coupled with this deep mysticism in matters of inner experience was a radical assertion of scientific rationalism regarding outer, sensory experience. The testimony of the senses must be yielded to on points of fact, and reason—natural reason—must be regarded as the proper instrument for determining unrevealed truth, while only with regard to supernatural truth were Scripture and the church decisive. Quoting St. Augustine and St. Thomas, Pascal proclaimed that any other position "would render our religion contemptible." Entering therewith upon the decisive issues of science and religion in his age, Pascal told the Jesuits that

it was to equally little purpose that you obtained against Galileo a decree from Rome, condemning his opinion respecting the motion of the earth. It will never be proved by such arguments as this that the earth remains stationary; and if it can be demonstrated by sure observation that it is the earth and not the sun that revolves, the efforts and arguments of all mankind put together will not hinder our planet from revolving, nor hinder themselves from revolving along with her.[3]

Thus at the end of this subtle argument about freedom and determinism, about predestination and grace, the victory

[2] See below, Chapter VI.

[3] Blaise Pascal, *The Provincial Letters* (Modern Library Edition; New York, 1941), Letter 18, p. 615.

of science over authority was triumphantly adduced. One must beware of assuming that the most rational and penetrating minds are somehow immune to the appeal of radically irrational views. As the case of Pascal demonstrates, the very intellectual despair of such superintellectuals gives birth to mysticism.

The mystical doctrine of the "inner light," which played such a significant role in the writings of Pascal, as it did in all of Jansenism, was the very center of the faith of the more radical Protestant sects of the sixteenth and seventeenth centuries. Their mysticism was not the peculiar possession of a select few, but the common heritage of all. If we define the word "mysticism" broadly to mean the certainty of conviction that one's own soul has achieved its goal of reality in God, then we might say that, like the Jansenists and Pascal, the sectarians of the inner light believed that there was something mystical and awe-inspiring in every man. This sense of mystery gave them the exalted quality which so troubled and exasperated their more rational contemporaries—a quality superbly illustrated in the personality of John Bunyan (1628–1688), author of *The Pilgrim's Progress*.

Both Luther and Calvin had been frightened by the anarchic consequences implicit in such radical doctrines and had sought to avoid these consequences by relying upon the prince (in Luther's case) or upon a pattern of theocracy (in Calvin's). Opposing all such authoritarianism, the mystic depended upon and lived by his direct communion with the Lord Almighty. The case of Jakob Böhme, a small shopkeeper of Silesia, may be taken as typical. In 1612 Böhme published a first account of his mystical visions under the title *Aurora*, claiming direct divine light as his source. Man, he argued, being compounded of spirit, soul, and body, must have a rebirth before he is able to achieve the true knowledge of God. He taught that God is all and nothing—he is the world-generating being which, from the bottomless abyss, projects a variety of essential phenomena, such as love and visible variety. The inherent difficulty of communicating the essential mystical experience is nowhere better illustrated than in Pascal's famous memorial of the night of November 23, 1654, in which he cried out, "Certitude, certitude, feeling, joy, peace, God of Jesus Christ . . . grandeur of the human soul . . . joy, joy, joy, tears of joy." Regardless of the poetical form in which the mystic clothed his experience, he would live in the fellowship which this experience created for him. It is one of the most characteristic features of this age that the worldly sense of power, manifest in such figures as Richelieu and Wallenstein, found its counterpart in a spiritual sense of power which animated Spanish Catholics as much as English "seekers," Jakob Böhme as intensely as Pascal or Kepler.

Such mystic ardor was a far cry from the sane and moderate rationalism of Richard Hooker (1553–1600), whose *The Laws of Ecclesiastical Polity* was perhaps the most balanced statement of the Anglican religious position and the most judicious defense of the established Church of England. But in the three generations which elapsed between Hooker's treatise, which appeared in the early 1590's, and the consummately skillful summary of English constitutional traditions penned by his admirer John Locke (published in 1690 as *Two Treatises of Government*),

Anglicanism was violently torn between a caesaro-papist Lutheranism and a strongly puritanical Calvinism.[4] Because of its later significance in the English revolution and the pioneering of the Pilgrim Fathers, the word "puritan" has been the subject of much confusion and abuse. It has no distinct theological meaning, but rather indicates a general attitude toward life which was found among Anglicans, Calvinists, and Sectarians alike. The most heatedly expressed controversy concerned problems of church government, but underneath these problems lay the explosive issues involved in predestination and free will. Calvinists generally, and Scottish Calvinists in particular, tended to push the predestinarian position to its radical extreme: there was no hope for anyone except those whom God had elected to be saved; all that men could do was to labor at their calling with all possible diligence and hope to catch a glimpse of the divine will through their efforts to contribute to God's greater glory. As Hooker put it, the Calvinists "disparaged" reason, and though they believed in an elite of the elect in heaven they were no respecters of earthly pomp and circumstance. It was a fierce and somber doctrine.

The Anglicans, on the other hand, inclined to side with the Thomist tradition, which, in the Reformed movement, had been most eloquently represented by Philipp Melanchthon (1497–1560) and by Jacobus Arminius (1560–1609), founder of the Remonstrant school of Reformed religion. What lay at the heart of the Remonstrants' position was their insistence upon freedom of the will and the consequent significance of manifesting one's Christianity through practical ethics. Strongly Humanist in its implications,

[4] See below, Chapter VI.

such a doctrine was more readily compatible with the refinement and civilized urbanity of the upper classes in England and the Netherlands than was the fierce challenge of predestination.

Spearheading the Protestant forces which opposed the advancing phalanx of the Counter Reformation were the Calvinists, forever haunted by their bitter concern with predestination. There was, at the same time, a distinct relation between some aspects of Calvinism and the rising spirit of science. It is well known that modern natural science is based upon the belief that there is some rational pattern inherent in nature and that it is the task of man to discover this rationality, to discover the laws or regularities which govern nature. This approach, stemming from Hellenic as well as Judaeo-Christian cosmologies, was clearly in accord with the Calvinist conception of God. Although the doctrine of the Trinity was retained, Calvin's God—one and decidedly only one—was predominantly a God of power, of majesty, and of will. This God, who created the universe according to inexorable and universal laws, had set before man the task of seeking to discover His laws and thereby of glorifying His power. These laws can be discovered only by a diligent observation of facts, combined with a determination to abstract from the details of observation in order to perceive regularities, regularities which may then be formulated as generalizations. "Generalization based upon observed matters of fact"—this key to the methodology of seventeenth-century science accorded well with Calvinist determinism and predestination. The piety in the face of nature's majesty which is so characteristic a trait of many great scientists served as an emotional underpinning for the scientists' scrupulous regard for factual evidence, because such evidence partook of that majesty.

"*The New Science*"

The century between the publication of Galileo Galilei's *Siderius nuncius* (1610) and *Letters on the Solar Spots* (1613) and Gottfried Wilhelm von Leibniz' *Monadology* (1714) was the most extraordinarily productive in the entire history of pure science. In mathematics, in astronomy, in physics, in chemistry, and in anatomy, physiology, and aspects of biology, man's knowledge advanced at a rate unparalleled before or since. In each of these fields the foundations were laid upon which the investigators of the next two centuries were to construct the familiar, but nonetheless awe-inspiring, edifice which we call "modern science." But what is important besides the particular contributions of any of the scientific giants of the seventeenth century, and the total increase in human knowledge for which they collectively deserve credit, is the development during this period of a certain outlook and of certain techniques which together constitute what is known as "scientific method." In this respect, the work of the seventeenth century represents nothing less than the culmination of a profound intellectual revolution, a revolution whose origins are to be found in the sixteenth century and whose effects are everywhere apparent in the twentieth.

The brilliant results of this outburst of scientific creativity should not be allowed to obscure one's view of the formidable obstacles that confronted the leading thinkers of the time, nor should the term "modern science" mislead one into the belief that these men were all agreed on the broad implications of their work. In spite of the growing scientific spirit of the seventeenth century, some of the worst witch-hunts belong to this period as the belief in sorcery and witches continued to prevail. In England, Scotland, and New England, as well as in Germany, Spain, and elsewhere on the continent, witches were burned and hanged by the hundreds. An overestimation of man's power was, generally, responsible for these superstitions, which were based upon the mistaken attribution of troublesome effects—such as sickness, madness, and death—to human agents. Is it too fanciful to suggest that in this baroque age, with its fantastic feeling of power as well as of insecurity, the very mystery that surrounded the startling discoveries of the men of science contributed to such outrages? Might not the revelation by these scientists of facts and relations hitherto undreamed of have led to increased credulity as well as to skepticism? Certainly it is true that the line between science and superstition seemed far less clear in the seventeenth century than it does today. The mystical belief in the aliveness and relatedness of all things in the universe, which served as a foundation for the great astronomical achievements of the mathematician Johannes Kepler (1571–1630), allowed him also to believe in astrology. The case of alchemy is similar; even the great Newton believed in it. Only by the slow spread of the scientific spirit, coupled with general enlightenment and broadening tolerance, did this scourge of superstitious belief in sorcery and witchcraft gradually subside.

But there were other traditional beliefs of a hallowed kind, notably the theologically supported notion that the earth was the center of the universe, which did yield to the onslaught of scientific advance in this period. In 1609 the

Italian scientist Galileo Galilei (1564–1642) learned that two Dutchmen had built a new instrument for magnifying man's vision, the telescope. He immediately began to build a similar but more powerful one. No sooner had he succeeded than his doubts about the Copernican heliocentric system were dispelled and he became a strong public advocate of the ideas of that Polish astronomer. Galileo's enthusiasm was that of one who is primarily concerned with observed matter of fact. For years he had struggled with the problems of motion, formulating the law of the acceleration of falling bodies. Experiment and calculation, factual observation, and daring hypotheses of rational interpretation—these together constituted the new scientific outlook. Because the factual observation was primarily quantitative, the hypotheses were of a very special kind. Measuring, counting, and weighing were the crucial methods; the refinement of the instruments employed for these tasks became a central concern of the scientist. Anyone who failed to appreciate the importance of the new outlook was considered old fashioned, a scholastic, and even a devotee of superstition.

Under the impact of the efforts of men like Galileo and Kepler, superstition acquired its modern meaning—the human tendency to believe explanations which are demonstrably contrary to established matter of fact or for which no observational basis can be adduced. The fight for science and against superstition, which began in the sixteenth century, was symbolized in Galileo's famous (though apocryphal) remark: "And yet it moves." These words were supposedly uttered as the scientist left the chamber where the Holy Inquisition had queried him concerning his Copernican teachings, forcing him to recant and admit that the earth did not move around the sun. "And yet it moves" became the battle cry of the antitraditionalist observer of the realities of nature who—in the interest of scientific truth—was ready to challenge everyone—pope, emperor, great council, and philosopher. Actually, this famous anecdote compresses into one brief incident what historically developed over sixteen years. As early as 1613 Galileo had raised the Copernican issue in his *Letters on the Solar Spots*, and three years later Pope Paul V ordered him not to hold or defend the proposition that the earth moved around the sun, a proposition that had been declared "heretical" by the theologians of the Holy Office. Sixteen years later, in apparent violation of this injunction, Galileo published his *Dialogue on the Two Great World Systems* (1632; *Dialogo dei due massimi sistemi del mondo*).[5] Examined by the Inquisition under threat of torture, the scientist recanted his objectionable teachings and was condemned to protective custody. But it was during precisely these years of enforced confinement that he produced the ripest fruit of his research, *The Two New Sciences* (1638). This testament of one of the greatest geniuses of the new scientific spirit set forth the principles of the "new science," the mathematical formulation of the observed regularities of bodies in motion. If less flamboyant than the immortal—and fictitious—remark flung in the teeth of the defenders of superstition, this work was Galileo's real answer to his obscurantist accusers.

Among the many workers in the field of the "new sci ence" there grew up after 1600 a sense of great mission.

[5] See Giorgio de Santillana's fine edition, with significant introduction (Galileo, *Dialogue on the Great World Systems*, Salusbury trans. [Chicago, 1953]).

The feeling of European unity was nowhere more pronounced than among these crusaders for a new world view; their voluminous correspondence strikingly anticipates the intellectual "cosmopolitanism" of the next century. Yet, among themselves, these men were sharply divided, not only on specific scientific issues but also on the broad philosophical basis of their work. The antagonism between Galileo's dedication to experiment and calculation and Kepler's more highly speculative mathematical approach was symptomatic of the age's preoccupation: should one try to ignore cosmological issues—"stay away from theology," as the Holy Father demanded of Galileo—or should one try to develop a new cosmology which would be compatible both with the new discoveries and with Christian theology?

John Donne (1573–1631), the metaphysical poet who throughout his life was deeply troubled by the "new philosophy" which "calls all in doubt," suggested the characteristically Protestant inclination toward the second alternative: "Methinks the new astronomy is thus applicable well, that we which are a little earth should rather move towards God, than that He which is fulfilling, and can come no wither, should move towards us." [6] This striking attempt to adapt the Copernican universe to the Christian religion would have been acclaimed by Kepler, who entertained similar ideas. Annoyed by Kepler's talk of "sentient souls" and "celestial harmonics," Galileo overlooked the fact that Kepler's *De harmonice mundi* (1619) also contained the third law of celestial motion, a law which established a connection between planetary periods and distances. On the other hand, Kepler's insistence on pursuing the

[6] Edmund Gosse, *Life and Letters of Dr. John Donne* (New York, 1899), I, 219–220.

will-o'-the-wisp of a "prime mover" (which he finally located in the sun) led him to ignore the most significant of Galileo's formulations, notably his law of acceleration. Thus two new basic lines of inquiry were kept apart by the philosophic antagonism of their most eminent exponents, and it remained for Sir Isaac Newton (1642–1727) to combine the two in his formulation of the law of gravitation as the key to the new cosmos, a formulation constructed out of the elements Kepler and Galileo had provided two generations earlier.

The Experimental Method: Bacon, Harvey, Boyle

Among the men who undertook to expound what they believed to be the philosophical implications of the new sciences, none is today more famous than the English lord chancellor, Francis Bacon (1561–1626). Although not himself a scientist of any distinction, Bacon was greatly excited by the immense strides which science had taken during his lifetime and dazzled by its potentialities for the future. A true son of his age, he believed that the chief glory of science lay in the fact that it increased the power of man; in his *Novum organum* (1620) he wrote, "Now the true and lawful goal of the sciences is none other than this: that human life be endowed with new discoveries and power." But in order for the sciences to attain this goal, it was, in Bacon's view, absolutely necessary that they follow the proper path; thus scientific *method* becomes crucially important. "The cause and root of nearly all evils in the sciences is this—that while we falsely extol and admire the powers of the human mind we neglect to seek for its true helps," he argued. "Neither the naked hand nor the understanding left to itself can effect much. It is by instruments and helps that the work is done, which are as much wanted for the understanding as for the hand." By "instruments" Bacon does not here mean primarily such devices as the telescope and the microscope, the slide rule and the logarithmic tables, all of which were developed during the seventeenth century. Rather, he refers to something that seemed to him much more fundamental; as the title of his *Novum organum* indicates, the "new instrument" is to be a system of rules provided for the guidance of the human mind in its search for truth. Taken together, these rules define the inductive, or empiricist, method.

Reduced to its essentials, Bacon's argument holds that the scientist must rid himself of all preconceptions and must turn, with a completely open mind, to a diligent study of the evidence presented by his senses. In practice, this profound suspicion of all prejudices, and indeed of all hypotheses as well, tended to lead to the mere amassing of factual data. Thus, when Bacon wished to discover the nature of heat, his method led him to compile lists of hot objects, of cold objects, and of objects of varying degrees of heat, in the hope of discovering some characteristic always present in hot objects and absent in cold. By contrast, his enthusiasm for experimentation was not informed by any clear grasp of what experimentation involves. Bacon explained the failure of the Greeks to develop any real science as the consequence of their mistaken notion "that the dignity of the human mind is impaired with long and close intercourse with experiments and particulars, subject to sense and bound in matter." Unquestionably Bacon's emphasis on the importance of "stubborn facts" and on the importance of the painstaking collection of concrete observational data served as a needed corrective for the excesses of sheer speculation in which some of his contemporaries engaged. But induction and experimentation represented only one side of the new science of men like Galileo and Newton; the other was mathematical calculation, and of this vital aspect Bacon showed scant appreciation.

Despite Bacon's great reputation, the weakness of his position was apparent to many of his contemporaries, and perhaps most notably to William Harvey (1578–1657), who observed wryly that "he writes philosophy [i.e., sciences] like a chancellor." Harvey was one of the greatest pioneers in experimental science, and his discovery of the circulation of the blood (described in his *Exercitatio anatomica de motu cordis et sanguinis*, 1628) was an outstanding example of how to record accurate observations, implement them with skillful experimentation and computation, and thus develop sound hypotheses based upon observed facts. His work, like Galileo's, was neither mere induction nor mere deduction, but a sound combination and blend of both. He shared Bacon's conviction that the evidence of the senses must always be preferred to received opinion and proposed "both to learn and to teach anatomy, not from books but from dissections, not from the positions of philosophers but from the fabric of nature." But, unlike Bacon, he recognized the importance of speculative reason in the formation of hypotheses. Harvey's description of his great discovery stands as a monument to the techniques of the new science, combining as it does elements of induction and deduction, as well as a reliance upon quantitative observation:

But what remains to be said upon the quantity and source of the blood which thus passes is of so novel and unheard-of character, that I not only fear injury to myself from the envy of a

few, but I tremble lest I have mankind at large for my enemies.
. . . Still the die is cast, and my trust is in my love of truth,
and the candour that inheres in cultivated minds. And sooth
to say, when I surveyed my mass of evidence, whether derived
from vivisections, and my various reflections on them, or from
the ventricles of the heart, . . . or from the arrangement and
intimate structure of the valves in particular . . . with many
things besides, I frequently and seriously bethought me, and I
long revolved in my mind, what might be the quantity of blood
which was transmitted, in how short a time its passage might be
effected, and the like. . . . [And] I began to think whether
there might not be A MOTION, AS IT WERE, IN A CIR-
CLE. Now this I afterwards found to be true; and I finally
saw that the blood . . . was distributed to the body at large,
and its several parts. . . . Which motion we may be allowed
to call circular.[7]

Fruitful though it might be in the hands of a man with
the imagination and insight of William Harvey, in the seventeenth century the experimental method was on the
whole most appropriate as an instrument of destruction.
As Pascal noted, one stubborn fact has the power to destroy
any general proposition, no matter how securely grounded
that proposition has previously been. But since the very essence of this experimental method is its healthy skepticism
of all theories, it has often been a positive inhibition upon
the creativity of its users. The case of the distinguished
chemist Robert Boyle (1627–1691), formulator of the law
of pressure in gasses, is perhaps the best example of this
aspect of the inductive method. An ardent follower of
Bacon, Boyle deliberately avoided reading the *Novum
organum* for many years, fearing that he might otherwise

[7] William Harvey, *The Circulation of the Blood* (Everyman
Edition; New York, 1923), pp. 55–56.

be "seduced" by his master's interpretations and fail to rely solely upon the evidence of his own senses. One can almost hear the lord chancellor's voice in Boyle's statement that "it has long seemed to me none of the least impediments of the real advancement of true natural philosophy that men have been so forward to write systems of it." Determined to escape this pitfall, Boyle struggled against his own strong inclination to accept the corpuscular view of the material universe. But in the long run even so orthodox a Baconian proved unable to operate successfully without some hypotheses to guide his experimentation, some "system" to give meaning to the concrete data which he had gathered; in the end, with many reservations and much hedging, Boyle espoused the corpuscular theory. Nevertheless, it is noteworthy that his most famous work, *The Sceptical Chymist* (1661), was significant primarily because it disavowed the Aristotelian theory of the four elements, thus preparing the way for the development of a truly creative science of chemistry during the next centuries.

The Deductive Method: Descartes, Hobbes, Spinoza

While Bacon and his followers stressed the inductive, experimental component of the new science, other men in the seventeenth century chose to emphasize its deductive, mathematical aspect. Although the most obvious difference between these two "schools" was one of practice, their views of the nature of the scientific method were also fundamentally at variance. We have already noted Boyle's criticism of the philosophers who had been too "forward" in writing systems; the contrast is indeed striking if one compares with this the criticism of Galileo's method put forward by the great French mathematician and philosopher, René Descartes (1596–1650): "He does not stop to examine all that is relevant to each point," Descartes wrote, "which shows that he has not examined them in order, and that he has merely sought reasons for particular effects, without having considered the first causes of nature; and thus he has built without a foundation." [8] What Boyle condemned as "system" was precisely the same thing that Descartes praised as "foundation"—namely, a comprehensive description and explanation of the universe, constructed by human reason on the basis of certain accepted first principles. In Bacon's view, such an intellectual system can only be constructed slowly (if at all) and as a result of the gradual accumulation of a vast body of data derived from experimentation and sensory experience. For Descartes the situation is completely reversed: one cannot know what use to make of the evidence presented by his senses, nor can he hope to experiment with any direction and purpose, unless he begins with a clear and distinct understanding of the nature of the universe. How, then, is one to arrive at such an understanding?

Like Bacon, Descartes took as his starting point a thoroughgoing skepticism of all received theories and dogmas; he saw no reason to accept these theories unless he could prove their validity to his own satisfaction. It is worth while to note the considerable intellectual arrogance implied by such a position, a position characteristic of most of the great intellectual figures of the age. Surely, these men possessed supreme self-assurance and unbounded confidence in their own intellectual powers; nowhere is this self-assurance more vivid than in Descartes' attempt to con-

---

[8] From letter to Father Mersenne (March, 1638); see *Correspondence*, ed. by C. Adam and G. Milhaud (Paris, 1941), III, 76.

struct the universe by sheer intellectual effort. Like an acrobat who scornfully removes all safety nets before performing his most daring feat, Descartes declared his determination to take nothing for granted, to doubt everything. But he then discovered, as he tells us in his *Discourse on Method* (1637), that it was impossible to doubt one thing —the very act of doubting. On this basis, he posited his famous proposition: *"Cogito ergo sum"*—I think, therefore I am. Having thus established his own existence as a doubting, thinking being, Descartes proceeded to deduce from this single certainty both the existence of God and the existence and nature of the physical universe. Briefly, he reasoned that the existence of a thinking being necessarily implied the existence of an infinite being, which is pure thought and which must be immortal and omnipotent, i.e., God. Thus:

When I turned back to my idea of a perfect Being, on the other hand, I discovered that existence was included in that idea in the same way that the idea of a triangle contains the equality of its angles to two right angles or that the idea of a sphere includes the equidistance of all its parts from its center. Perhaps, in fact, the existence of the perfect Being is even more evident. Consequently, it is at least as certain that God, who is this perfect Being, exists, as any theorem of geometry could possibly be.[9]

Similarly, since man is conscious of an external world, and since this consciousness can come neither from man's own mind nor from God, the external world must in fact exist. It is a world of matter, as distinguished from both the self

[9] René Descartes, *Discourse on Method*, tr. by Lawrence J. Lafleur (New York: Liberal Arts Press, 1956), pp. 23–24.

and God, which are spirit, and consequently it can only be grasped by the human mind through the categories of space, time, and cause. Thus, in the Cartesian system the only sure knowledge of the material universe is mathematical knowledge; the evidence of the senses can never be trusted.

If (to use Francis Bacon's image) the experimental scientist is like an ant, assiduously gathering grains of evidence in order to construct his world, then the deductive scientist is like a spider, spinning webs of deduction out of his own rational being. In this spiderlike rationalistic process, mathematics, and particularly the techniques of geometry, played a crucial role. It should come as no surprise that Descartes was himself among the most distinguished mathematicians of his age. His discovery of analytic geometry (with Pierre de Fermat, between 1630 and 1640) and Pascal's work on probability theory were the most decisive developments prior to Newton's and Leibniz' work on the differential and integral calculus later in the century. Descartes' approach to geometry (and to mathematics in general) may be called dynamic, in contrast to the static approach of classical Greek mathematicians. He observed geometrical figures in the process of becoming, so to speak, rather than contemplating them as fixed verities. And from his work in mathematics he derived habits of mind, and deductive techniques, which he then applied to all scientific and philosophical problems. This effort to deal scientifically with the first causes of nature, to apply mathematics to the universe, led to the proud rationalism of Descartes' assertion, in his *Principia philosophiae* (1644), that "there is no phenomenon in nature which has not been dealt with in this treatise." Descartes' exaggerated sense of the power of the mind was in its very emphasis typically and dramatically baroque.

The same extreme reliance upon logical deduction from "self-evident" first principles is to be found in the philosophizing of Thomas Hobbes and of Baruch Spinoza, respectively the authors of a politics and of an ethics *more geometrico* (in the manner of geometry). Hobbes did not consider himself a follower of Descartes. Unappreciative of Descartes' mathematics (which he presumably did not understand), and sharply hostile to Cartesian metaphysics, Hobbes proceeded to make a radical effort to interpret man and the state as mechanisms. It is curious that a man of his acumen should have considered himself working in the tradition of Galileo and Kepler when he wrote *De cive* (1642), *De homine* (1658), and *Leviathan* (1651), followed by *De corpore* in 1655. He assumed throughout these works that matter and motion are the principles by which *all* events may be explained, stating in the *Leviathan:* "Seeing life is but a motion of limbs, the beginning whereof is in some principal part within; why may we not say that all Automata (engines that move themselves by springs and wheels as doth a watch) have an artificial life?" In this respect Hobbes obviously went far beyond Descartes. If Descartes had spoken of the body as a "machine," Hobbes completely rejected Descartes' sharp distinction between body and soul and insisted that psychology must be studied as a branch of physics (mechanics) and that it was grounded upon mechanical principles. Hobbes consequently was a radical determinist, believing that all man's employment of the will, so-called, is the result of his perceptions, which in turn result from the impact of external causes.

The principles of mechanics are the principles from which all is derived. Although Hobbes was aware of the limits of the deductive method, he also distrusted mere observation and induction in the manner of Bacon. Thought, he believed, must be combined with observed fact to produce scientific insight. The laws of motion constitute the general laws of nature, and since all change consists in motion, therefore "all happens in nature mechanically." By this metaphysical proposition Hobbes subverted the very essence of the scientific work of such men as Galileo and Harvey. But having made this extraordinary assumption, he proceeded to work out a deductive "proof" of the mechanistic premise, as well as of the axiom of inertia. Basing his argument on the same mechanistic premise, Hobbes held that all thought was simply calculation. Furthermore, defining calculation as adding and subtracting, he maintained that all things when transformed into thought could be so added and subtracted. "Reason," we learn from the *Leviathan*, "is nothing but reckoning, that is adding and subtracting, of the consequences of general names agreed upon for the marking and signifying of our thoughts."

In presenting such a proposition, Hobbes made himself the highly representative, although perhaps exaggerated, expression of his age. But, like Bacon and Spinoza, his mathematical ineptitude prevented him from appreciating the philosophical limits of any mathematics of the infinite. Unlike Kepler, Descartes, and Pascal, whose mathematical genius made them realize the strictly formal nature of the mathematical insight and led them to recognize the remain-

ing substantive problems of existence, Hobbes greatly overestimated the value and the applicability of mathematical
insights. Nor did he really understand the value of experimentation. Introspection, implemented by an unproven
major premise that all men are like Thomas Hobbes, was
the basis of his psychology and the politics derived from it.
What resulted from such an approach we have discussed
in Chapter I. The most extreme pantheistic position was
developed later in the century by the Dutch lens grinder,
Baruch Spinoza.

Both Spinoza and Hobbes were hotly attacked by their
contemporaries as atheists. When plague and fire swept
through London in 1664 and 1665, superstition once again
raised its head. In 1663 Descartes' writings had been put
on the Index, and in 1664, like the witch-hunters on a lower
level, divines and parlementarians combined to silence the
impious voice of Hobbes.

It was not an innovation that organized, rational religion
should fight the deviations into mysticism and naturalism;
not only in the Middle Ages but throughout the sixteenth
and earlier seventeenth centuries the struggle had gone on,
and it was not restricted to any one particular church. If
the Anglican divines were after Hobbes, the Lutheran pas-
tors persecuted Kepler and Böhme, the Calvinist orthodoxy
exiled Grotius, the Jews ousted Spinoza from their congre-
gation, while the Holy See pursued Galileo and the Jesuits
attacked Pascal, Descartes, and the nuns of Port Royal and
their learned guests. But these proceedings have often
puzzled men of later ages. Not only did Spinoza seem to
Goethe to have been the man "drunk with God," but
surely Kepler, Pascal, Böhme, and Descartes were, each
in a different key, strongly religious men animated by a

deep sense of awe for what the philosopher Kant was to describe as the two most profound sources of wonder, "the starred heavens above and the moral law within."

The passionate concern of the age with nature and its secrets, and its persistent doubting of all human authority, was fed by what seems to us now a faith of extraordinary depth and intensity—a faith in God's power to order the universe and a corresponding faith in man's power to understand this order and in the light of his understanding to master nature and to order anew man's life on earth. Mysticism, pantheism, and naturalism were all logical outgrowths of elements in the older Christian orthodoxy, both Catholic and Reformed. When Bacon wrote in his *Advancement of Learning* (1605) that he would separate metaphysics from the "first philosophy" and treat it as part of natural science, he added that he would subdivide the inquiry into causes "according to the received and sound division of causes; the one part which is physic inquires and handles the material and efficient causes; and the other which is metaphysic and handles the formal and final causes."

Descartes' thinking ran along similar lines, although he was troubled lest one meddle with matters beyond one's understanding. "Finally we shall not seek for the reason of natural things from the end which God or nature has set before Him in their creation; for we should not take so much upon ourselves as to believe that God could take us into his counsels." For, in Descartes' opinion, God's will is the basis for the entire world and all the permanent laws governing it, laws which reason may discover. As one commentator has said, "The supreme truth, the basic axiom, is that God exists." Pascal, animated by an intensely personal experience of God, found this Cartesian God little more than an empty abstraction; though a first mover, this God was dangerously close to being a pantheistic deity which becomes submerged in nature.

It remained for Spinoza, using the severely deductive method of geometry, to formulate such an all-engulfing pantheism. In his *Short Treatise on God, Man and His Well-Being* (probably composed in 1659–1660), Spinoza based his argument on the propositions that: (a) God exists, (b) God is a being of whom all or infinite attributes are predicated, of which every one is infinitely perfect of its kind, and (c) God is the cause of all things, and from this total causation were derived the doctrines of his providence and predestination. A completely deterministic universe resulted in which "the big fish devour the little fish by natural right":

For as God has a right to everything, and God's right is nothing else, but his very power, as far as the latter is considered to be absolutely free; it follows from this, that every natural thing has by nature as much right, as it has power to exist and operate; since the natural power of every natural thing, whereby it exists and operates, is nothing else but the power of God, which is absolutely free.[10]

It was Spinoza's glory that he pursued to the bitter end the implications of the Cartesian philosophy and its mathematical and physical antecedents. Only in our own time have the practical implications of such a conception come fully into view. The God whose quintessence is power, who is the cause of all events in a nature which is itself a congeries of power relations, is a curious expression of the dual trend

[10] Benedict de Spinoza, *Tractatus Politicus* (London, 1909), ch. ii, pp. 291–292.

toward mysticism and skepticism which pervaded religion, philosophy, and science during an age whose poets included Donne as well as Shakespeare, Calderón, and Milton. In that age the world-view of the modern man took definite shape and organized itself for the conquest of mankind. Whether this was a glorious achievement or a disastrous betrayal of human destiny seems more controversial today than at any time in the intervening three hundred years.

The Rational Universe: Newton and Leibniz

In the spring of 1687 a weighty, highly technical treatise was published in London; its title was *Philosophiae naturalis principia mathematica*, its author Isaac Newton (1642–1727), professor of mathematics at Cambridge University. In this book Newton described in mathematical terms the laws which govern the motion of every body in the universe—from the falling apple and the tides on earth to the planet in its orbit. Many parts of the Newtonian system had been anticipated by earlier scientists, notably by Kepler, Galileo, and Christian Huygens (1629–1695), as well as by three Englishmen, members of the Royal Society who had worked on the problem of gravitation—the astronomer royal, Edmund Halley (1656–1742), Robert Hooke (1635–1703), and Sir Christopher Wren (1632–1723). But in the *Principia*, for the first time, their isolated explanations of phenomena in astronomy and terrestrial mechanics were made part of a mathematically precise, coherent, and elegant theoretical synthesis. In the words of a modern historian, the Newtonian synthesis "represented the culmination of the scientific revolution and established the basis of modern science." Perhaps even more important than Newton's contribution to man's understanding of the universe, however, was the fact that he finally established and popularized the canons of the modern scientific method. In this connection it is worth while to note a famous passage from the third book of the *Principia:*

Rule I. We are to admit no more causes of natural things than such as are both true and sufficient to explain their appearances. . . .

Rule II. Therefore to the same natural effects we must, as far as possible, assign the same causes. . . .

Rule III. The qualities of bodies, which admit neither intensification nor remission of degrees, and which are found to belong to all bodies within the reach of our experiments, are to be esteemed the universal qualities of all bodies whatsoever.

For since the qualities of bodies are only known to us by experiments, we are to hold for universal all such as universally agree with experiments. . . . We are certainly not to relinquish the evidence of experiments for the sake of dreams and vain fictions of our own devising; nor are we to recede from the analogy of Nature, which is wont to be simple, and always consonant to itself.[11]

Although experimentation and the evidence of the senses were central in Newton's method, as evidenced especially in his work in optics, he also discovered a mathematical method of describing and measuring motion—the so-called "calculus," which applied algebra to motion as Descartes had applied it to geometry. Like Galileo, Newton wedded the experimental and the deductive method, creating an intellectual instrument of unprecedented scope and power.

[11] Isaac Newton, *The Mathematical Principles of Natural Philosophy;* selection from *The Autobiography of Science,* ed. by F. R. Moulton and J. J. Schifferes (New York: Doubleday and Company, Inc., 1946), pp. 186–187.

Newton's system, like those of most truly great intellectual figures, represented both an end and a beginning. On the one hand, as we have seen, it came as a fitting climax to two centuries of intense scientific endeavor. On the other hand, it set the stage for the major religious, philosophic, and scientific developments of the next centuries. Indeed, it is almost impossible to overemphasize the influence of Newton and his work, an influence that still persists in our own day despite the fact that Newtonian physics has recently been superceded. Although the picture of an orderly, rational universe governed by immutable laws had inspired scientists long before Newton's time, the popular acceptance of such a picture is due largely to his reputation. When Alexander Pope wrote the famous couplet

> Nature and Nature's laws lay hid in night:
> God said, Let Newton be! and all was Light,

he was simply expressing the almost universal opinion of his age. Thus the significance of the *Principia* was not confined to the world of pure science; on the contrary, Newton stood as a symbol of the rationality of the universe and of the power of man to discover its laws. The supposed "lesson" of Newtonian science was applied promiscuously to every area of human activity. Building upon very real advances in statistical knowledge, the Englishman Sir William Petty (1623–1687) undertook to develop a *Political Arithmetick;* in the preface to this book, written in 1683, he described his proposed method:

For instead of using only comparative and superlative words, and intellectual Arguments, I have taken the course (as a Specimen of the Political Arithmetick I have long aimed at) to express my self in Terms of *Number, Weight,* or *Measure;* to use only Arguments of Sense, and to consider only such Causes, as have visible Foundations in Nature; leaving those that depend upon the mutable Minds, Opinions, Appetites, and Passions of particular Men, to the Consideration of Others.[12]

A detailed account of the ramifications of the Newtonian world-view belongs properly to a history of the eighteenth century.[13] But the story of the age of power would be incomplete without the towering figure of Gottfried Wilhelm von Leibniz (1646–1716). The last European thinker who mastered the whole of knowledge, this puzzling and extraordinary philosopher dealt at one time or another with mathematics, the natural sciences, theology, history, politics, jurisprudence, and philology. At the same time, he was a statesman and diplomat who pursued the goal of universal peace. As a philosopher, he was not systematic; he never wrote a "great work," and to this very day his philosophy must be pieced together from a profusion of fragments and occasional essays. Of these, two are especially well known: the *Theodicy* (1710) and the *Monadology* (1714), written for Prince Eugene of Savoy. In the *Theodicy*, Leibniz defended the view that

it is a consequence of the supreme perfection of the Sovereign of the Universe, that the kingdom of God be the most perfect of all possible states or governments, and that consequently the little evil there is, is required for the consummation of the immense good which is there found

[12] The reader might note the way in which Petty echoes the passage from the Wisdom of Solomon quoted at the opening of this chapter.

[13] See Frank E. Manuel, *The Age of Reason* (Ithaca, N.Y., 1951), ch. ii.

—a view made famous by the merciless satire to which it was subjected in Voltaire's *Candide*. In the *Monadology*, Leibniz argued that all substance is composed of particles which he called "monads"; these particles, which are in essence energy, are neither material nor spiritual:

In God there is *Power*, which is the source of all, also *Knowledge*, whose content is the variety of the ideas, and finally *Will*, which makes changes or products according to the principle of the best. These characteristics correspond to what in the created Monads forms the ground or basis, to the faculty of Perception and to the faculty of Appetition. But in God these attributes are absolutely infinite or perfect.[14]

Leibniz shares with Newton the distinction of having discovered (quite independently) the calculus, and it has recently been noted that he anticipated many of the principles of modern mathematical logic. But it is in his central concern with power and in his combination of rationalistic and empirical techniques that he is most representative of his age. At the same time, his theoretical and moral program was such as to make him, according to Ernst Cassirer, "the true originator and founder of the philosophy of the Enlightenment."

These philosophical trends correspond to the evolution in theology. Here the men known as "deists" sought to establish the relation of God to the rational, mechanistic universe revealed by the new natural science. Harking back to the efforts at reconciliation made by Lord Herbert of Cherbury (1583–1648; especially in his *De veritate*, 1624) and by Hugo Grotius, the deist position found its most celebrated exponent in John Locke. It was not really a re-

[14] G. W. von Leibniz, *Monadology* (Oxford, 1898), ¶ 48, pp. 244–245.

ligious movement, but rather an attempt to adjust traditional religious belief to the growing secular spirit and
rational speculation. Strictly speaking, deism is the position
that natural theology and rational morality are the essence
of religion. Stripping away such "superfluous" details as
miracles, prophecy, revelation, and ritual, the deist con-
ceives of God as a distant but benevolent prime mover,
who created the world-machine and who then conveniently
stepped out of the picture, leaving man to order his life
by the light of his natural reason. How deeply this trend
was embedded in the main philosophical developments of
the time may be gauged by reflecting upon Pascal's bitter
comment on Descartes: "I cannot forgive Descartes. In
all his philosophy he would have been quite willing to dis-
pense with God. But he had to make Him give a fillip to
set the world in motion; beyond this, he had no further
need of God." [15] However unjust to Descartes' undoubted
theism, this is the reaction of an intensely religious mind to
the secularizing propensity of the age of power.

[15] Blaise Pascal, *Pensées* (Modern Library Edition; New York,
1941), sec. II, no. 77, p. 29.

CHAPTER IV

The Thirty Years' War

IT HAS been the fashion to minimize the religious aspect of the great wars which between 1618 and 1648 raged over the territory of the Holy Roman Empire of the German Nation in the heart of Europe. Not only the calculating statecraft of Cardinals Richelieu and Mazarin but even the explicit statements of Urban VIII (pope, 1623–1644) gave support to such a view in a later age which had come to look upon religion and politics as separate fields of thought and action. Liberal historians were to find it difficult to perceive that for baroque man the most intensely political issues were precisely those raised by religion. Gone was the neopaganism of the Renaissance, with its preoccupation with worldly self-fulfillment. Once again, and for the last time, life was seen as meaningful in religious, even theological, terms; the greater insight into power which the Renaissance had brought served merely to deepen the political passion brought to the struggle over religious faiths.

Later ages, incapable of feeling the religious passions which stirred baroque humanity and much impressed with the solidified national states which the seventeenth century bequeathed to posterity, were prone to magnify the dynastic and often Machiavellian policies adopted by rulers who professed to be deeply religious and therefore to deny the religious character of these wars. But it is precisely this capacity to regard the statesman as the champion of religion, to live and act the drama of man's dual dependence upon faith and power, that constituted the quintessence of the baroque. The Jesuits, sponsors of the baroque style in architecture, advised Catholic rulers concerning their dual duties; what the Catholics did elicited a corresponding pattern of thought and action in the Protestant world. The somber and passionate driving force behind so much unscrupulousness was religious pathos in all its depth.

The Origins

Since what is commonly called the Thirty Years' War was in fact a series of wars lasting from the revolt of Bohemia in 1618 to the Peace of Westphalia in 1648, it is in some respects misleading to speak of "the origins" of these wars as though they all stemmed from a common source. In fact, as we shall see, each of the four distinct wars which mark this era had its own origins. Nevertheless, the term Thirty Years' War is not without meaning; distinct though they were, all these wars did reflect the pattern of European politics and religion in the first half of the seventeenth century. It is of this common background that we must speak before discussing the wars themselves.

At the beginning of the seventeenth century the division of Europe into opposing camps animated by religious belief was not, in itself, sufficiently clear-cut or profound to lead to a general conflagration. True, each side had its extremists —the militant orders of the Jesuits and Capuchins among the Catholics, the Calvinists among the Protestants—but the animosities within each camp were almost as great as those between them, and as yet few men were prepared to contemplate a holy war designed simply to exterminate heretics. Indeed, dynastic politics, "reason of state," often completely obscured the lines of religious division, as in the case of the Catholic Henry IV of France (1553–1610), who simultaneously collaborated with the pope and the Dutch Republic to advance the interests of the House of Bourbon, and who was about to make war on the Hapsburg emperor Rudolf II (1552–1612) in league with the Protestant princes of Germany when his life was cut short by the assassin François Ravaillac. Nevertheless, the uneasy balance between the forces of the Reformation and those of the Counter Reformation made the peace of Europe increasingly precarious, while domestic conflicts in England, France, the Netherlands, and the territories of the Holy Roman Empire demonstrated anew the power of religion to move men to passionate action. In these sultry years a great European war of religion was an ever-present possibility; only two things were needed to make it a reality: a further structuring of existing antagonisms and an issue which would crystallize opinion on both sides. Both were provided during the fateful decade 1608–1618, within the territories of the tottering Holy Roman Empire.

The first decisive step toward the wars of 1618–1648 was the formation of rival alliance systems—the Protestant Union and the Catholic League—by the Protestant and the Catholic estates of the empire in 1608 and 1609. Though not formally concluded until 1609, the Catholic League had been long advocated by its foremost protagonist, the distinguished statesman and military leader, Duke Maximilian of Bavaria (1573–1651), as the only method for stem-

ming the tide of Protestant progress throughout Germany.
His appeals were primarily directed toward the princes of
the church whose position was patently threatened by the
continuous extension of Protestantism. As duke of Bavaria,
Maximilian was faced with the problem of how to buttress
and defend the Catholic position in Germany without sacri-
ficing his sovereignty to imperial pretensions; the League,
from which Austria was excluded, was his instrument for
effecting this purpose. It provided him with a broad foundation for Catholic leadership and created a counterpoise to
the power of Hapsburg. In this crucial position, Maximilian
characteristically avoided various grandiose but risky
schemes and was content to build slowly and steadily so as
to be prepared for any eventual conflict. As director of the
League and commander of its forces, he occupied the foremost place among the Catholic princes in Germany apart
from the Hapsburgs.

No such clear-cut leadership and direction proved possible among the Protestants. Indeed, their religious convictions as well as their practical interests were diversified to
the point of serious conflict. Hence the establishment of the
Union was the product of common fears rather than
common aims, and its eventual employment for effective
action remained more doubtful. Lutherans and Calvinists
fought each other with much venom, the former being passive and conservative, the latter active and progressive. As
might have been expected, the main pressure in favor of the
Union came from the Calvinist princes of south Germany,
at first the elector palatine (Frederick IV, 1574–1610) and
later the elector of Brandenburg (John Sigismund, 1572–
1619). In the actual negotiation of the agreement, however,
certain south German Lutheran princes played a leading

part. They had been deeply stirred by the vigorous proceedings, in 1607, of Maximilian of Bavaria against a small south German town, Donauwörth, and had come to feel that Protestant interests in Germany would thereafter have to be defended by force of arms. The Protestants decided to establish a common treasury and to set up an armed force, under the leadership of the elector palatine. Consequently, in 1610, the Protestants of Germany faced the Catholics as one armed camp against the other.

Each group allied with foreign powers, the League with Spain and the Union with France and England, and the stage was set for a European conflagration. But it took ten more years until the spark was set to this tinderbox. Nor did the conflict originally break out between members of the two camps; both were drawn into a conflict between crown and estates, between Catholicism and Protestantism, in Bohemia. Amid all the complex detail of the internal politics of the several Hapsburg realms, two forces stood out in bold relief: the conservative Catholic policy of the House of Hapsburg and the progressive Protestant efforts of the several estates. There were of course more than a few Catholics in the estates' assemblies, but the Protestants were dominant and continued to gain adherents, except where checked by the determined efforts of their prince. The House of Hapsburg had farmed out, so to speak, the several subdivisions of its far-flung possessions to younger sons, called archdukes. In some of these constituent parts, the power and privileges of the estates, usually composed of lords, knights, and burgesses, had become much more considerable than in others; this was especially true in Hungary and Bohemia. In the latter, the states had secured the Letter of Majesty (Sovereignty) in 1609—a formal agreement limiting the sovereignty of the prince and eliminating the famous rule of *"Cujus regio, ejus religio"* which provided that a man must confess the religion of the established authorities in the territory in which he lived.[1] According to this new agreement, complete religious equality and freedom were to prevail in Bohemia. Though the provisions were broadly drawn, they left plenty of openings for further controversy, as we shall see. Here as elsewhere it is difficult to say whether the religious conflict brought about the demand for political rights on behalf of the estates, or whether the surge toward political participation enhanced the appeal of the new religion. Undoubtedly a close connection existed; yet the constitutional division of power between princes and estates had existed for a long time. Only when the new religion had appeared did the problem of supremacy present itself. Since the monarchical exponents of Catholicism were united in the House of Hapsburg, it was natural that the estates of the several realms should seek to combine to further their claims. Hence the estates of Bohemia, Silesia, Moravia, Hungary, and Upper and Lower Austria formed a series of leagues which in turn sought to collaborate with the Protestant estates of the empire, more particularly as represented by the Protestant Union. These negotiations, never quite conclusive, had a threatening portent. Through such an alliance, the civil war which began in 1618 in Bohemia spread to the whole decaying structure of the empire.

Ever since the Golden Bull of 1365 had been issued by Charles IV, king of Bohemia and Holy Roman emperor,

---

[1] The origins of *"cujus regio, ejus religio"* are obscure. It is commonly (though wrongly) believed to have been formulated by the Diet of Augsburg in 1555; its intimate, though to modern eyes startling, tying of religion and government had been the basis of the empire's tenuous peace.

Bohemia had remained a vital part of the empire. During the two and one-half centuries that had elapsed by 1617, Bohemia had been one of the richest of the Hapsburg possessions north of the Alps and Pyrenees. The Bohemian people, both Czech- and German-speaking elements, enjoyed considerable freedom, especially in matters of religion. Yet, in spite of the predominantly Protestant sentiment of the country, the Hapsburg rulers Rudolf II and Matthias (1557–1619) had favored Catholics for the chief offices of state, and the more ardent elements in the Catholic group were anxious to press for further advance against the Protestant position. For example, at Braunau, a Catholic prelate had on a questionable pretext seized a Protestant church and attempted to compel Protestants to attend Catholic services.

The crisis which was finally to plunge Europe into the devastating thirty years of war arose over the issue of the succession to the Bohemian throne. In 1617, although the childless Matthias was still alive, both Catholics and Protestants began to cast about for likely candidates for his Bohemian throne. Among the Protestants, Lutheran opinion inclined toward the elector of Saxony (John George, 1585–1656), while the Calvinist and Hussite factions definitely preferred the young elector palatine, Frederick V (1596–1632). The Hapsburgs, on the other hand, had settled upon Ferdinand of Styria (1578–1637) as the most appropriate successor; chosen largely because he had children, Ferdinand had a record of ardent Catholic sympathies. A pupil of the Jesuits, he had made every effort to restore Catholicism in Styria, while at the same time reducing the position of the estates to the minimum. Such a man was likely to be more unwelcome in Bohemia than either Rudolf or Matthias. Nevertheless, when Matthias precipitated the issue by calling for the selection of a king-elect on June 17, 1617, the large majority of Protestants in the estates, under weak and divided leadership, timidly voted for Ferdinand. They then insisted upon Ferdinand's guaranteeing the Letter of Majesty, which he did, not because he intended to keep it but for "reasons of state." Thus the stage was set for a violent clash between estates and king.

On August 28, 1619, after long negotiations, Ferdinand was unanimously elected to succeed Matthias as Holy Roman emperor, as he had succeeded him on the Bohemian throne two years earlier. Several days before, however, on August 19, the confederated estates of Bohemia, Silesia, Moravia, and Lusatia had declared him deposed. The events which led up to this dramatic culmination were essentially three: there were the religious incidents already alluded to, which provided the background; there were arbitrary acts of the government infringing the Letter of Majesty by unilateral action; and there were the several moves by which the estates countered the royal actions, more especially the celebrated defenestration of Prague the year before (May 23, 1618), when two unpopular councilors were bodily thrown from a window of the emperor's castle to a moat sixty feet below. Throwing imperial councilors out of a window, even though they lived to tell the tale, constituted open defiance and revolution, and it was so interpreted by all—by the immediate participants, by the Bohemian people, and by Europe at large. The Thirty Years' War had begun.

The Bohemian War

The Bohemian revolutionaries, having deposed Ferdinand, proceeded to set up a provisional government. To Count Henry Mathew of Thurn, the spirited but conceited leader of the radical elements, was given the command of the Bohemian forces; Ernst Mansfeld, captain of mercenary troops, illegitimate scion of a princely house, and self-made count, had been transferred to the service of the Bohemians by Charles Emmanuel of Savoy on the promptings of Christian of Anhalt, who may well be considered the directing genius of the revolutionary movement. An ardent Calvinist and a somewhat unprincipled practitioner of "reason of state," Anhalt was the key councilor of the young elector palatine. Unfortunately the weaknesses of the one compounded those of the other. The elector, a charming, decent prince but a weak and unmilitary man, had won the hand of Elizabeth, the daughter of James I of England, in 1613. It was upon this fact alone that Anhalt built many unsound hopes. More persuasive than sound, and much inclined to construct elaborate projects on speculative assumptions rather than on known facts, Anhalt consistently underestimated the inertia, envy, and mutual jealousy of most men and overestimated their attachment to ideal causes, more especially the cause of Protestantism. Handicapped by his youth and inexperience, the elector palatine was not the man to deal with so dynamic a personality as Anhalt. Hence the Palatine party, despite the devotion of their immediate adherents, failed recurrently at decisive moments.

Anhalt, unwarned by the failure of his earlier project of having Frederick elected king of Bohemia instead of Ferdinand, chose to revive this scheme when the revolutionary estates were casting about for a new king. When the elector of Saxony refused their overtures, the estates did in fact elect Frederick, who, after some hesitation, accepted. It is ironic in the light of later happenings to read his Declaration: "Moreover we considered that if we came to reject this rightful calling, the effusion of much blood and the wasting of many lands must have been laid to our account." [2] If Frederick had been tough, if he had taken the gamble for what it was worth and had demanded that the electing estates make sure of the kingdom which they were offering, while he himself secured the defenses of the Palatinate, he might possibly have succeeded in staking out a claim of lasting value. Instead he went to Prague as if the kingdom were secure, only to find himself unsupported by the estates in the vital matter of ways and means for the maintenance of an army able to defend the kingdom against the combined forces of the Hapsburgs and the Catholic League. For the League of Catholic princes, ably led by Maximilian of Bavaria, had the dual interest of monarchical legitimacy and the extension of Catholic Christianity to unite them against the Bohemian revolutionaries.

The imperial election in 1619 produced a double debacle in which Ferdinand II was informed of the loss of his Bohemian crown almost simultaneously with his election to the imperial throne, and Frederick learned that his vote as elector palatine had been cast for Ferdinand just as he was seizing the new emperor's Bohemian throne. By this comedy of errors Ferdinand had become emperor at the moment his Protestant enemies were on the point of gaining the decisive vote in the Electoral College and Frederick had, by proxy, acknowledged Ferdinand emperor at the same time that he was seizing his crown in Bohemia. This catastrophic confusion was decisive in the sense that it alarmed all Europe and thus set the stage for the long bloody struggle which was to follow; yet the Bohemian campaign itself was short. After some indecisive operations in 1618 and 1619, the ac-

[2] Quoted by C. V. Wedgwood in *The Thirty Years' War* (New Haven, 1939), p. 67.

tual declaration of war—the imperial demand to Frederick to quit Bohemia by June 1, 1620—was followed by one Protestant setback after another, culminating in the complete rout of the Bohemian forces at the battle of the White Mountain (November 8, 1620). Frederick, when apprised of this disaster, decided to abandon Prague and retreat. Having failed in his attempts to rally Silesia or Lusatia to his cause, the "Winter King," as Frederick was now called in mocking reference to the brevity of his effective reign, started on a tour of the courts of Europe in the vain hope of persuading them to support his Bohemian venture. In the process of maintaining his claim upon the Bohemian crown, he lost in the end even his German principality of the Palatinate.

The Catholics, with the momentum of their victories and the full backing of the imperial authority, began to liquidate their enemies. In Bohemia the revolutionaries suffered penalties of prison and death, followed by confiscations of their property on such a vast scale that it is believed half of all important landholdings changed hands. Not only in Bohemia, but in the Palatinate and elsewhere, the Jesuit Order then moved in, taking over schools and universities, proscribing Protestant clergy and teachers, and forcing the people to attend Catholic services. Finally, in 1623, a general settlement was made. It was not truly a peace, any more than the later treaties of Lübeck (1629) and Prague (1635). Maximilian of Bavaria was given the electoral vote previously exercised by Frederick, and four years later he received the Upper Palatinate and the Lower Palatinate, east of the Rhine; the Lutheran elector of Saxony obtained control over Lusatia for his aid in subduing Bohemia. By these acts, the two most important princes of the realm suggested that theirs was a policy of personal aggrandizement, even as they headed their respective coalitions of Catholic and Protestant princes. Of these, the Bavarian move was to prove the more obviously disastrous, since it blocked the road to peace and kept the determined adherents of the elector palatine at work seeking support for a restoration of Frederick. Thus the very terms that ended the Bohemian war virtually guaranteed that the peace of Europe would not long endure.

The Danish Phase

While the House of Hapsburg and its allies settled down to the task of reconverting to Catholicism the lands they had conquered, the Protestants inside Germany, and more especially the supporters of the elector palatine, Frederick, cast about for some new source of support with which to challenge the outcome of the Bohemian war. James I of England having failed the Protestant cause, and the Dutch being heavily committed against Spain after the lapse of the armistice between those two powers (1621), the anti-Hapsburg diplomats turned to the Scandinavian kingdoms of Denmark and Sweden, where two able and ambitious rulers, both of whom, although of native descent, were related by their German mothers and wives to Germany, had come to the throne in recent years: Christian IV (1577–1648) in Denmark, and Gustavus II Adolphus (1594–1632) in Sweden. Each was to enter the Thirty Years' War, but not at the same time. Their marked rivalry, which had already flared up into open war (1611–1613), stood in the way of a joint enterprise. In addition, and perhaps even more importantly, Gustavus II Adolphus was at this point occupied in a protracted conflict with the kingdom of Poland, whose crown he claimed.

Christian of Denmark, whose possessions in Holstein made him a prince of the German empire and who had become head of the military forces of the Lower Saxon District of the empire, maintained that he took up arms against the emperor because of the latter's unconstitutional actions toward the elector palatine. For Christian the religious issue was clearly less important than the struggle for political power, although for the people at large religion remained a vital issue, as, indeed, it did for Ferdinand.

Christian's intervention in the war was, like the Bohemian phase, a story of almost unrelieved Protestant defeats. The imperial forces, taking advantage of their vastly superior resources, were able to avoid decisive engagements during the summers of 1624 and 1625 and to allow their mercenary troops to live off the land. Then, as Catholic prospects brightened in 1625, the emperor received vast new support from an unexpected source: Albrecht von Wallenstein (1583–1634), soon to be made duke of Friedland, undertook to put an army of 24,000 into the field, to arm and equip them, and to come to the support of Johan Tserclaes Tilly (1559–1632), the League's general. Wallenstein's appearance altered Christian's position materially and caused him in the spring of 1626 to dispatch part of his forces under Mansfeld to Silesia, in the hope of diverting Wallenstein to the defense of the Hapsburg dominions proper. The strategy failed as Wallenstein split his forces and defeated Mansfeld at Dessau (April 25, 1626), while Christian was routed by Tilly (at Lutter am Barenberge in August 1626). Having crushed the Protestant forces in the east and having driven Christian back to his duchy of Holstein, Wallenstein raised an even larger army, said to have numbered 70,000 men, and set forth once again to annihilate the Danish king and secure control of the Baltic for the empire. After an eminently successful campaign, Wallenstein's army was halted by the resistance of the free city of Stralsund in Pomerania during the summer of 1627. This act of resistance provided enough of a counterpoise to permit a settlement with Christian.

After several months of negotiation, a peace was concluded at Lübeck on May 22, 1629. Christian not only received back Jutland, Schleswig, and his part of Holstein, but escaped the expected indemnity. In return for these material concessions he renounced all claims to German territory as well as the directorship of the Lower Saxon District. It was because of new and greater dangers, especially those threatening from Sweden, which in the meantime had come to terms with Poland, that Wallenstein had urged, and the emperor accepted, these surprisingly moderate terms.

The Edict of Restitution

Even before peace was concluded with Denmark, Ferdinand II had taken a step much at variance with Wallenstein's concept of imperial absolutism but dear to the heart of the emperor and expressing his religious convictions. On March 8, 1629, he issued the Edict of Restitution. The Edict, without sanction or discussion by the diet or Reichstag of the empire, as required under the constitution in all matters of major legislation, proclaimed all alienation of church lands since 1552 null and void, called for their restitution to the rightful proprietors, authorized the latter after such restitution to expel all who would not confess according to the preference of the ruler of the territory, and, with the exception of the Lutherans of the Augsburg Confession (1530), outlawed all Protestant confessions and especially the Calvinists. For the enforcement of the Edict, imperial commissioners were authorized; against their decisions there was no appeal. In concrete terms, this meant not only the re-establishment of archbishoprics, bishoprics, and monasteries in territories by then largely Protestant, but also the expulsion of tens of thousands of peaceful and industrious citizens.

Ferdinand, by this arbitrary and nonconstitutional act, had overreached himself. As events were soon to show, his attempt to undo the development of three generations was the high-water mark of imperial power and Catholic reaction. The Edict convinced even the most pacifically inclined Protestant princes that the house of Hapsburg meant to destroy the ancient constitution of the empire and the "liberties" of the German people, institutionalized as they were in the rights and privileges of princes, of knights and burghers, of electors and free cities, in short, of all the estates of the empire save his own. They realized that, if the balance was to be redressed, even foreign intervention must be countenanced in order to cope with so formidable a threat. Sweden and France, Gustavus II Adolphus and Richelieu, stood ready to take advantage of the situation.

The Edict of Restitution and the war between the House of Hapsburg and France over the succession to the duchy of Mantua (1627–1631) set the stage for the electoral gathering at Regensburg as it assembled in early July 1630. The results of this meeting, perhaps a reflection of the skillful diplomacy of Richelieu and his emissary Father Joseph, proved highly favorable to the French policy of sowing discord between the emperor and his electors: Wallenstein was dismissed from his post as imperial general; Ferdinand was unsuccessful in his attempt to obtain the election of his son to the imperial throne; and a further breach was caused over the Edict of Restitution, as Brandenburg and Saxony refused to adhere to it, but agreed only on a further meeting to discuss it.

That Ferdinand should have assented to the dismissal of Wallenstein, and that a majority of his council should have favored such a step, shows them to have been basically unaware of the trend of the times. In Ferdinand's case, it was partly weakness, partly perhaps a desire to reassert his imperial authority over his victorious but willful general, and partly a dissatisfaction with Wallenstein's indifference toward the religious cause; he had opposed the Edict of Restitution and had enforced it only where it fitted into his broader political strategy. In a historical hour, Ferdinand opted for religion and mediaeval conceptions of government, while Louis XIII at the very same time resisted all pressures along similar lines and retained Richelieu—who like Wallenstein was prepared to subordinate all, including religious considerations, to the requirements of royal absolutism. Implicit in these decisions was a struggle between the French idea of the state and its *raison d'Etat* and the mediaeval constitutionalism of the empire, in which the cardinal and his monkish emissary, taking full advantage of their opponents' inner divisions, faced the emperor and his electors. These constitutional issues, however, were soon obscured by the startling successes on the battlefield of a new and brilliant commander, King Gustavus II Adolphus of Sweden.

The Swedish Challenge

Gustavus II Adolphus had already been king of Sweden for nineteen of his thirty-five years when he landed in Germany on July 4, 1630. Most of that period he had spent in protracted wars in which he had defeated his neighbors Denmark, Russia, and Poland. Descendant of the native line of Vasa kings, Gustavus represented in modern garb the hoary idea of the Germanic warrior king, ruling and leading his people in battle by right of the intrinsic authority derived from a supreme capacity for leadership. Yet Gustavus II Adolphus was a genuine pathfinder of the modern national state.[3] Hostile to the aristocracy, who quite recently had hoped to convert Sweden into a "republic" ruled by the nobles as Poland was, this sturdy champion of the Protestant cause had carried forward the work of establishing a centralized administrative state and a productive industrial society and had succeeded in professionalizing his army to an extent astonishing for the period. By bringing his army into the German war, Gustavus II Adolphus provided a genuine counterpoise to the Spanish professionals supplied to the Catholic side by the senior branch of the House of Hapsburg.

Aided by substantial support from the French, Gustavus met with immediate success; within six months he had won control of most of Pomerania and was threatening Brandenburg. These victories merely whetted the appetite of the Swedish king, who believed himself divinely appointed to smash the power of Hapsburg and the antichrist forever,

[3] See below, Chapter VII.

and he had no hesitation in concluding at Bärwalde (January 13, 1631) a five-year treaty with Richelieu's ambassador, providing for the advance of an army of 36,000 Swedes into Germany to rescue the German estates and their "liberties." These German liberties had been a French concern for almost a hundred years; in keeping with the adage "divide and conquer," the French were happy to provide Gustavus with a susbidy of 400,000 thalers in support of the cause. This strong French backing, plus the shock and indignation caused in Protestant Europe by the destruction of the city of Magdeburg (May 20, 1631), won for Gustavus the support of virtually every Protestant prince in the empire. Ever a believer in the decisive battle, he sought and found the forces of the enemy commanded by Tilly in the broad plain north of Leipzig and won a decisive victory at Breitenfeld (September 7, 1631).

Filled with multifarious—military, political, and administrative—activities as was Gustavus II Adolphus' year of triumph between the battles of Breitenfeld and Lützen, three only were of major importance. The first was his project for a Protestant confederation (*corpus Evangelicorum*) under Swedish leadership, and the second, on the failure of the first, was his proposal for a general peace. This too having failed, Gustavus found himself faced, in the spring of 1632, by the superior forces of the newly reinstated Wallenstein. To break Wallenstein's armed camp and general strategy of attrition became the king's third objective. Honoring his agreement with John George of Saxony, Gustavus pursued Wallenstein, who had invaded Saxony in the hope of forcing the elector to abandon the Protestant cause, and had made the egregious error of splitting his forces for better wintering. After a fierce struggle near Lützen, southwest of Leipzig, on November 6, 1632, he utterly routed the imperial armies, but the king himself lost his life upon the battlefield. The magnificent campaign, which in so many ways resembled the meteoric conquests of Alexander the Great, thus came to a dramatic close.

The fact that the Swedish armies did not dissolve on the battlefield on which their king fell demonstrated that unlike his rival Christian of Denmark, Gustavus Adolphus was no lone wolf. He left not only very able military lieutenants, but also the sagacious chancellor Axel Oxenstierna, who had worked with and under him. Largely as a result of the loyalty and determination of Oxenstierna, the Protestant cause was upheld in the face of repeated defeats long after its leader's death.

The months between the death of Gustavus and the battle of Nördlingen (September 1634) were dominated by the intrigues of Wallenstein, who conducted secret (indeed, impenetrable) negotiations with the Saxons, the Swedes, and the French. Whatever his aim may have been, Wallenstein succeeded only in estranging himself from the imperial court; in February 1634, having been condemned for treason in a secret imperial conclave, he was murdered. Wallenstein's very contradictions, contrasts, and tensions reflected his true nature. Somber and highly dynamic, in keeping with the style of his age, he elicited universally those intense emotions of admiration and hostility which only such a truly representative figure is capable of arousing. Indeed, how else could one imagine Wallenstein departing this earth than by an exit as tragic and dramatic as a great state murder? Combining mediaeval faith and superstition with a Renaissance sense of power and artistic performance, baroque man was forever walking upon a stage:

European history was a theater and the beauty of a performance was enhanced by a dramatic exit for its hero. Results were incidental.

Wallenstein's death once more raised hopes of a general peace, but instead Protestants and Swedes suffered an overwhelming defeat in the battle of Nördlingen. Thus the Swedish phase of the Thirty Years' War came to an end almost exactly three years after Gustavus II Adolphus' victory at Breitenfeld had seemed to open the prospect for a victory of Protestantism. The five battles of the White Mountain, Lutter am Barenberge, Breitenfeld, Lützen, and Nördlingen were the turning points of the great war; after Nördlingen many a bloody engagement was fought, but none again altered the direction of events as these had done. The inner weakness of the cause of the Counter Reformation is dramatically revealed in its failure—in spite of losing only two of these great encounters—to win the war in the end, and that failure can be explained only in terms of the forces of the modern state which were predominantly on the other side.

French Intervention and the Peace of Westphalia

The abortive Treaty of Prague (1635), which from the outside looked more like a defensive alliance among the German estates than a treaty of peace, increased the Swedish and French determination to reduce the Hapsburg power further and to secure extensive compensations for their sanguinary and financial efforts up to that time. Richelieu in particular believed that the time had come to launch the final assault upon Hapsburg power and, if not utterly to destroy it, in any case to reduce it to the point where it could no longer threaten the imperial ambitions of

France. From the time of the first French intervention in 1631, the Thirty Years' War had become less and less religious in character, and when Richelieu in 1635 finally acknowledged his policy with a formal declaration of war upon the Austrian Hapsburgs, "reason of state" and power politics had completely superseded spiritual concerns. In early battles with Spanish forces attacking from their base in the Netherlands, the French suffered a series of defeats; but gradually the tide of war changed. In due course, the internal weakness of Spain, highlighted by the successful revolt of Portugal in 1640, was revealed in a crushing defeat by the French at Rocroy (1643), which ended the legend of the invincibility of the Spanish infantry. Spain lost almost 15,000 men and never recovered from the disaster.

The preliminaries of a peace which had actually been under negotiation since about 1641 finally took definite shape with the emperor's authorization after Rocroy. At about the same time, two new rulers, Queen Christina of Sweden (1626–1689) and Pope Innocent X (1644–1655), lent support to the cause of peace, while the Dutch, having decided that France was a greater threat than Spain, welcomed the start of negotiations. In fact, the very real obstacles to peace derived not from any continuing will to fight on the part of the participants but from the innate complexity of the situation. Since some of the German estates were on their side, both France and Sweden insisted that they were at war with the Hapsburgs, rather than the empire. For their part, the estates insisted upon participation in the negotiations, not only to protect their territorial rights, but also to settle the constitutional and other internal issues which the war had originated; under the constitution of the empire these were issues of immediate concern to them. In the face of these complications, it became necessary to divide the problem into two parts and physically to separate the relevant negotiations so that the treaty between the Austrian Hapsburgs with their allies and France was drawn up at Münster, while at Osnabrück, some miles away, the Swedes negotiated with the empire and its estates. If this procedure made negotiation possible, it also made it slow and clumsy. In addition two other factors contributed to the great length of time required to complete the agreements. One was the fact that a number of powers that may or may not have participated in the fighting but were not directly concerned in the treaty, such as Spain, the United Provinces, Portugal and Venice, Denmark and Poland, were nevertheless brought into the negotiations. The other, and perhaps more serious difficulty, resulted from failure to arrange for a cessation of hostilities while the congresses met. For five years the parties wrangled, maneuvered, and shifted at Münster and Osnabrück, living in plenty while the surrounding countryside starved and while terrible destruction was wrought upon the helpless mass of the people, not only in Germany, but in Italy, France, and elsewhere.

The main political and territorial provisions of the treaty, now generally known as the Peace of Westphalia of 1648, were as follows: each German principality was declared a sovereign member of the body known as the empire and hence could declare war and make peace at its own discretion; Switzerland and the United Provinces, formerly bound to the empire by a shadowy dependence, were accorded the status of full sovereignty; France was ceded Alsace, and her forcible acquisition of the bishoprics of Metz, Toul, and Verdun was confirmed; Sweden acquired the western parts of Pomerania and secured control of the mouths of the three great German rivers (the Weser, the Elbe, and the Oder); Brandenburg, starting on its career of expansion, added most of eastern Pomerania and three bishoprics to its possessions; within the empire, Calvinists were given equal status with Lutherans. The treaty, since its terms precluded objections by the church, was inevitably condemned by Pope Innocent X; but even though this ban was never lifted, the treaty became and remained a symbol of the emergence of the modern state and of the system of many such states, facing each other as strictly secular sovereigns. The protracted struggle of the Counter Reformation to recapture the unity of Christendom by force of arms had ended in failure.

From every point of view, the Thirty Years' War was an unmitigated catastrophe for Germany, while at the same time it utterly failed to achieve its original religious objectives. The actual physical destruction, even after allowing generously for the inaccuracy of earlier figures, cannot but stagger the imagination. In Württemberg, to choose an extreme case, the number of men capable of bearing arms had dropped from 65,400 to 14,800 in twenty-nine years (1623–1652), and more than half of all buildings had been destroyed (318 castles, 36,100 houses in the cities). In long-range terms, however, the institutional confusion caused by the perpetuation of a vast array of principalities large and small was perhaps even worse. It could only serve to prevent the growth of a suitable government and constitution and the development of a healthy national spirit. In terms of the religious objectives, the high hopes of Ferdinand II and his Counter Reformation associates were finished, as were the Calvinists' projects for a predominantly Protestant empire. The formula "*Cujus regio, ejus religio*" was reaffirmed, and, in a negative sense, religion triumphed over politics in the struggle for control of the emerging national states. The Peace of Westphalia produced in each kingdom, duchy, and principality of the empire a version of the modern state but in no case was it a full vigorous manifestation of the creative implications of the age. Too often it was a crippled, barebones "state," a mere apparatus—a bureaucracy serving princely aspirations for aggrandizement and power. The nation remained outside. For the next two centuries the future belonged to the successful national states that were being created in France, England, and elsewhere.

CHAPTER V

France: Absolute Power

THE French monarchy of the seventeenth century, created above all by the conscious efforts of a single man, Armand Jean du Plessis, duc de Richelieu (1585–1642), and supremely embodied in the person of Louis XIV (1638–1715), the *Roi Soleil*, was both the most admired and the most widely copied government of its time. No detail of its structure or appearance was too trivial to be noted and emulated throughout Europe. It is reported that the elector Frederick III of Brandenburg was so convinced of the perfection of Louis XIV's court that, although he was quite happily married and a devoted husband, he "added to his establishment a lady who had the title and court functions, though not the pleasures, of being his mistress." [1] From Stuart England to the Russia of the Romanovs, from the vigorous reforms of Gustavus II Adolphus and Oxenstierna in Sweden to the tarnished splendors of Bourbon Spain, absolute monarchy was in the ascendant. In taking France as their model, the rulers of the age were paying a deserved tribute to the first great example of the modern, secular state—that institution which, more than any other, has molded the life and the history of the last three centuries.

[1] Clark, *op. cit.*, p. 91.

If any single day may be called the birthday of the modern state it is probably November 10, 1630, the famous "day of dupes" on which Richelieu finally outmaneuvered the queen mother, Marie de Médicis (1573–1642), in their struggle for the confidence and support of the young king, Louis XIII (1601–1643). Marie had demanded that her son dismiss the prime minister, but at the decisive moment, when Richelieu had shrewdly offered his resignation, Louis uttered these crucial words: "We are not concerned with the queen mother. I honor my mother, but I am more obligated to the state than to her." In these words the king acknowledged himself the state's servant, thus confirming the victory of the impersonal state over the personal feelings and loyalties which ruled feudal society as well as private men. Barely five years later, in defending Richelieu against the criticisms of the *parlement* of Paris, Louis vigorously reaffirmed the absolutist conception of government when he said, "It is none of your business to meddle in the affairs of my state and I forbid you to assume to be my tutors in so meddling with the affairs of state." My state! This cannot but suggest the famous royal exclamation: "I am the state," which even if apocryphal, summed up perfectly the identification of the monarch Louis XIV with the mysticism of the national body corporate, the state, "*l'Etat.*" To this day Frenchmen write the word with a capital, the only French common noun so honored. We must examine the striking series of events that led to this dramatic conclusion.

Richelieu and Louis XIII

It will perhaps seem strange, in a chapter devoted to the form of government known as absolute monarchy, that the name of Richelieu should be given precedence over that of his king. Yet it could hardly be otherwise, for despite the *mystique* of monarchy, the "divinity" that "doth hedge a king," there can be no doubt that the minister was the dominant member of this partnership. Richelieu was forty in 1624 when he achieved the position of supreme power which he held till his death in 1642. Although of weak physical constitution, he was a man of superb intellectual ability and overweening ambition, of cold, calculating ruthlessness and tremendous energy and tenacity. Motivated by deep but controlled passions, Richelieu possessed a superb political imagination, based on a penetrating knowledge of man—a species he generally despised.

Richelieu, in his celebrated *Political Testament*, described his policy as compounded of three interrelated parts: destroying the Huguenots' opposition to the French monarchy, reducing the great nobles to the status of subjects, and raising the royal prestige and power at home and abroad to its deserved place in the sun.[2] These were really different aspects of one central objective: the development of the independence of the royal power at home and abroad into true sovereignty. Louis XIII, in spite of his limited ability, had the judgment to recognize Richelieu's contribution to the royal power and prestige and supported him accordingly. And Richelieu, by the achievement of "absolute" power for the king, correspondingly enhanced his own position. The great minister's objective or plan was thus as simple as only a superb strategist of political power could conceive and carry out. Though a prince of the church, he formulated the absolute claims of secular authority and established the body corporate of the modern

[2] Richelieu, *Testament politique*, ed. by Louis André (Paris, 1947), p. 95.

state. Thus out of numerous beginnings and origins reaching far back into the Middle Ages, the state emerged from the hands of this builder, a model, whether admired or feared, to be copied by all. If the state, as Machiavelli had believed, was the most admirable work of art man can make, Richelieu's creation emerged a true example of baroque style, embodying as it did the characteristic ambivalence of spiritual and secular forces, a supreme secular institution created by a prince of the church.

The first of Richelieu's three aims—the destruction of Huguenot opposition—was, characteristically, dictated by political rather than religious considerations. Although he was a cardinal of the Roman Catholic Church, not a single one of his acts can be explained solely in terms of religious motivation. In this case, it was the anomalous position of the Huguenots within the French state, and not their heretical beliefs, that determined Richelieu to act. Under the Edict of Nantes (1598), which had resolved the protracted religious wars of the previous century (1562–1598), the Calvinists had emerged as a recognized and protected minority. The higher nobility and the citizens of a number of cities and towns, including some fortified ones, were not only given the right to Protestant worship, but they could hold public office and participate in four of the *parlements* or provincial high courts. After the death of Henry IV in 1610, moreover, the Huguenots, not content with these guarantees, had made common cause with the aristocrats in their efforts to destroy all vestiges of centralized political power and to substitute a political organization similar to the Holy Roman Empire with the country divided into districts, each having a military force and captain of its own. Since the more radical preachers had used the frequent Cal-

vinist assemblies to stir up action, Louis XIII exacted an
agreement, after their defeat in 1622, not to meet without
his leave. But they soon violated this promise, asserting that
it had been given conditionally and on the premise that the
king would fulfill his part of the bargain. Especially important to them was the fact that a fort threatening the city
of La Rochelle, one of their three remaining strongholds,
was actually being built up. The Huguenots quite correctly
suspected that Richelieu intended the destruction of this
key city; in fact, Richelieu had told the king in a secret
memorandum that his position and crown could not be considered secure while part of his subjects constituted a state
within the state and that therefore La Rochelle must be
conquered. Perhaps from a sense of impending doom, perhaps because they counted on receiving aid from the Protestant English and Dutch, the Huguenots precipitated the
issue in the autumn of 1624 by themselves rising against the
royal authority.

The ensuing conflict, in which the Huguenots, led by the
duc de Soubise and his brother the duc de Rohan, actually
received support not from the Protestant powers but from
Catholic Spain, is of little intrinsic interest. In spite of Spanish aid, the Huguenots suffered setbacks on all sides and
eventually sued for peace. The more ardent Catholics, of
course, wanted to see them utterly crushed; but Richelieu
refused to go further than a compromise. The peace of La
Rochelle (February 1626), negotiated by the English, was
the result; one suspects that Richelieu had no intention of
keeping it. In any case, both the crown and the Huguenots
immediately started violating its terms, on the ground that
the other party was planning to do so. The appearance off
La Rochelle in July 1627 of a British fleet carrying 5,000

men signaled the beginning of the final conflict; since Richelieu's diplomacy had allied France with Spain and had neutralized the Dutch, the British, under the impetuous duke of Buckingham,[3] were the Huguenots' sole hope. Buckingham's repeated failures to relieve the city and Richelieu's brilliant strategy of isolating it from the sea by erecting a wall across its harbor sealed the fate of La Rochelle. Completely cut off from outside supplies, and with its population reduced from 25,000 to 5,000, this last stronghold of French Protestantism surrendered unconditionally to the king in October 1628. Once again Richelieu counseled moderation; but while the pitiful survivors were granted their lives, their possessions, and the right to exercise their religion freely, the essential autonomy of the city, as of so many others throughout the breadth of Europe, and more especially of France, was destroyed. The proud independence of La Rochelle had rested upon its privileges, more especially upon its local self-government. All that was now gone; the modern state triumphed with its officials and tax collectors; the walls and towers were razed never to rise again.

The achievement of Richelieu's second objective—the subjugation of the great nobles—was, as we have seen, intimately associated with the destruction of the Huguenot opposition. Ever since the Reformation had first raised the religious issue, the broad tendency of politics had been to divide France into two camps, one Protestant (Calvinist), feudally aristocratic, and anti-Spanish, and the other Catholic, royalist-bureaucratic, and pro-Spanish. It was the strategic genius of Richelieu to transcend this traditional partisanship and to weld together the royalist-bureaucratic

[3] See below, Chapter VI.

and the anti-Protestant *and* anti-Spanish positions and to
make of the combination one solid foundation for the unity
of France, her power and preponderance under an absolute
monarch. Thus the close co-operation between the Huguenots and the aristocracy, as well as the support which the
Spanish gave the Huguenots in their ill-fated revolt, played
directly into the hands of the skillful cardinal; he could
now take full advantage of the anti-Protestant, anti-Spanish,
and proroyalist sentiments of the rising bourgeoisie. The
key to the successes of Richelieu and the monarchy during
this crucial period is to be found in the decisive fact that,
as in England under the Tudors, the middle class was for
the king and the state.

This allegiance of the middle class was, in turn, only par-
tially explained by prejudice against Spain or Protestantism
or by monarchical sentiments; the fact is that the middle
class recognized the superior efficiency of the king's government and realized the advantages which it might bring
them. Thus in the last analysis the striking successes of
Richelieu's policy of strengthening the state internally and
externally turned upon his unflagging detailed attention to
certain key problems of administration. Under his watchful
eye, the army, the government service or bureaucracy, the
navy, commerce, and shipping all underwent the sort of
rationalization which twentieth-century engineers and efficiency experts like to call "streamlining." It was a passion
of the age, oddly at variance, so it seems at first glance, with
the baroque world of theatrical display, the grand gesture
and the involved intrigue, but in fact born of the same
limitless dynamism and love of power. Technique now first
detached itself from all higher purposes and became an end
in itself. In Richelieu's mind the state was not, as it had

been for Machiavelli, a work of art through which ancient virtue or manliness might find its most noble expression; it was an instrument designed for the achievement of many complex and interrelated purposes. If its first objective was to make France great and prosperous, it was to enable her and her king to become the successful champions of the Counter Reformation and to serve at the same time as the stage upon which Armand Jean du Plessis, duc de Richelieu, could play out his drama of the monk within this world—severe, disciplined, and yet at the same time majestic, powerful, rich beyond the dreams of avarice.

Richelieu recognized more fully than most that the armed forces, both on land and sea, were the backbone of power; and what is more, he realized that unless these forces were freed from feudal dispersion of responsibility and were centrally controlled, they were of little value. This, of course, was the prevailing view of the age—Spain, the Netherlands, and Sweden had each created a remarkable professional military establishment, and others followed—but here as in so many things Richelieu's greatness lay in carrying what was generally recognized to its ultimate and radical conclusion. As early as 1626 he had urged the creation of a standing army of 20,000 men. Many of the methods which had to be worked out in this period—regular pay for each soldier, discipline and a chain of command without hereditary officers to interfere, regularized provision of food, quarters, and clothing—have since become commonplace. Even more striking, perhaps, than these efforts in the military field were Richelieu's determination and enterprise in creating a navy. When he arrived in power, the French navy was controlled by great nobles who inherited the title of admiral and who did no more than they chose; under

Soubise it had actually been used by the rebellious Huguenots. The cardinal therefore had himself made "grandmaster, chief and superintendent general of navigation and commerce" (1626), abolished the admiralships (1627), and immediately set about creating a royal navy of thirty vessels which, with maintenance, cost 1,500,000 *livres* per year, "so that [the king's] neighbors will have the consideration they should have for a great state."

The one field in which Richelieu's achievement was less than impressive was public finance. Although the state of France's fiscal affairs was lamentable when he came to power in 1624, it was considerably worse at the time of his death. The pattern was the one usual in cases where poor management is combined with active government: both income and expenditures increased regularly, but the latter increased so much more rapidly that the gap between them grew ever wider. By 1640 the *interest* on the public debt was substantially larger than the total income of the government had been in 1626. The tremendous spread between what was collected from the unhappy taxpayer—the burden of taxation was notoriously uneven—and what the state received was one of the clearest signs of the rottenness of financial administration under Richelieu, for customarily only about half of what was collected became available to the state. It should be added, however, that this shocking situation was by no means simply the result of the prime minister's carelessness or his financial incompetence; to a considerable extent it resulted from a deliberate choice on his part. Richelieu did not believe that the activities of a state, and particularly its external affairs, should be limited by the resources immediately available to it, nor did he suffer a man to work under him who would have had the strength of character to insist upon such a view. His maxim was: "For no sum of money is the safety of the state too dearly bought." Hence his willingness to offer millions to Gustavus II Adolphus and others at a time when his treasury was empty.

Richelieu's third aim—raising royal prestige and power abroad—was perhaps closer to his heart than either of the other two, although it was clearly inseparable from, and dependent upon, them. Only a strong and unified nation could fill the place which the cardinal wished to achieve for France. In 1631 Richelieu entered upon the most aggressive and successful phase of that foreign policy, which was to leave him arbiter of the fate of Europe. France's position, like his own personal existence, was maintained by high *esprit* and indomitable will power and presented the inspiring spectacle of a nation glorying in its hegemony over Europe—the most brilliant baroque masterpiece of the age.

On December 4, 1642, Richelieu died, according to his historian "the greatest public servant France ever had"; his king, whom he had served so forcefully and effectively, followed him a few months later on May 14, 1643. The greatness of this genius in politics, ruthless and without pity either for himself or for others, was intuitively perceived by his contemporaries, even when they hated and opposed him. To them as to us he was a striking symbol of the patent fact that the great men of politics are often evil. Upon his death, his witty, friendly rival, Urban VIII, trenchantly remarked, "If God exists, he will probably have to atone; if not, he was a good man." Richelieu carried all the pathos of high ecclesiastical office into the new secular devotion to the religion of nationalism and its organization, the state, which he substituted for allegiance to Christianity and church. No doubt, like his great contemporary, Descartes, he considered himself a good son of the church; no doubt, either, that he built the instrument with which it could be superseded.

Mazarin and the Fronde

When Louis XIII died, his son, the future Louis XIV, had not yet reached his fifth birthday; for the next nine years the widowed queen, Anne of Austria, was the nominal ruler of France. Actually, during the eighteen years between 1643 and 1661, France was ruled by Richelieu's chosen successor, the Italian-born Cardinal Mazarin (1602–1661). The intimate relations between the queen regent and her prime minister—often rumored to have been a clandestine marriage—soon gave Mazarin actual control of the affairs of the kingdom to an even greater extent than Richelieu had enjoyed during his most powerful periods.[4] Using his power to the utmost, and relying heavily upon the talents of such military leaders as the prince de Condé (known simply as "the Prince," 1621–1686) and the vicomte de Turenne (1611–1675), Mazarin carried on the active and aggressive foreign policy of his predecessor. As we have seen, French participation in the Thirty Years' War was brought to a successful conclusion by the favorable terms of the Peace of Westphalia; meanwhile the war with Spain continued after the breakdown of negotiations in 1646.

[4] The comte de Saint Aulaire characterizes this as "the most frank, the longest, and above all the most fertile collaboration that history records between a sovereign and her prime minister" (*Mazarin* [Paris, 1946], p. 71).

Indeed, the most decisive event of the period, which occurred within France, was touched off by the failure of
Mazarin to conclude the peace with Spain.

As the struggle against absolutism progressed in England,[5]
the French nobility, high and low, as well as the urban
aristocracy, were once again stirred into resentment over
the loss of their mediaeval constitutional rights. Because the
Estates-General had not been convened since 1614 and
there was no constitutional way to force the monarch to
call them, the provincial high courts (*parlements*) undertook to make themselves the spokesmen of the more vocal
elements of the population. Although the focal point of the
crisis was the terrible suffering of the common people of
France, the leaders of the Fronde, as the opposition to the
monarchy was called, were selfish men at heart, devoid of
those deep ideological concerns which animated the English
revolutionaries of the time. Indeed, there prevailed a light-
hearted frivolity among the Frondeurs which well justified
giving the whole movement the name of a game the children
played in the crowded streets of Paris. In brief, the Fronde
was essentially an alliance among the great nobles of France,
taking advantage of the widespread unrest and discontent
caused by the stringent taxes which Mazarin had imposed
in order to prosecute the war against Spain. The civil wars
which wasted so much of the soil of France in the years
1649–1652 resulted rather from a revival of feudal notions
of resistance by the landed aristocracy in support of their
own privileges than from a constitutional revolution such as
was at the same time being fought out across the English
Channel. National unity and the centralized secular government which are symbolized in the word *Etat*, the modern

[5] See below, Chapter VI.

national state, were being obstructed by Frondeurs of all ranks. Unlike their English contemporaries, they did not accept this state and seek to constitutionalize it; they rejected it in the name of the law of a bygone feudal society and refused to listen to the reason which would refashion the law to make it suit an emerging new society. The Frondeurs enthroned absolutism in France by their failure to reform constitutionalism.

After the inevitable defeat of the Fronde, one great enterprise remained for Mazarin to bring to an end—the Spanish war. The ups and downs of this conflict need not be traced here; slowly French military and economic superiority wore down the Spaniards' will to fight, until in 1658 they initiated negotiations. The terms of the Treaty of the Pyrenees (1659), while falling short of Mazarin's most extended ambitions, were favorable to France, breaking finally the stranglehold of the Hapsburgs on her eastern borders. But when one considers the treaty as a whole it becomes clear that its specific provisions were overshadowed by the striking reversal in the relative positions of the two rivals as France took the place of Spain as the foremost European power. If in the long run this change proved to be decisive, it was at the time made palatable to the proud Spaniards by the marriage of Louis XIV and the infanta, Maria Theresa, which made the concessions appear almost like a dowry. Spain fought long and hard to prevent the marriage from implying that the French king had gained a right of succession to the Spanish throne; but since this concession was made conditional upon the regular payment of the dowry, and since this soon was in default, the treaty actually laid the groundwork for the extended wars of the next generation, notably the War of the Spanish Succession.[6] Mazarin, now at the height of his political and personal power, did not long survive his striking achievement; he died on March 9, 1661. After all is said and done, his two most important bequests to the generation following were the pacification of France and Europe and the preparation and training of a king and minister capable of carrying on: Louis XIV and Colbert.

The Sun King

On the day following the death of Mazarin, the twenty-two-year-old Louis XIV became the sole and absolute ruler of the kingdom of France. In 1643 he had succeeded his father on the throne, but now, eighteen years later, he became "the king who governs his state," not merely the king who reigns over it. To symbolize this change, Louis summoned to him the chief officers of state and members of his court and announced his firm intention to supervise every action of his government; when the president of the assembly of clergy inquired to whom he should in the future address himself, the king replied, "To me." In his *Memoires*, written for the instruction of his son, Louis was equally explicit: "Above all," he declared, "I was resolved not to have a prime minister and not to allow another to perform the functions of the king, while I would retain nothing but the title. On the contrary, I wished to apportion the execution of my orders among several persons, in order to unite all authority in myself alone." [7] This determination to be a king in fact as well as in name required, if it was to be translated into reality, a truly prodigious effort. Louis

[6] See below, Chapter VII.

[7] *Memoires de Louis XIV*, ed. by Charles Dreyss (Paris, 1860), II, 385–386.

XIV recognized this fact and was willing to pay the price of being an absolute monarch; it is reported that on a typical day the young king presided over the Council of Finance from ten in the morning until one-thirty, dined, presided over another council, secluded himself for two hours to study Latin, and, in the evening, attended a third council until ten o'clock. It should not be supposed, however, that the Sun King looked upon this as unmitigated drudgery. On the contrary, he felt his royal profession was "grand, noble and delightful." Passionately enamoured of glory himself, he created around himself at the court of Versailles the most glorious and majestic spectacle of the century. As a great French historian has put it: "Not only for his own time, when kings imitated his palace, his court, his person, his gestures, his entire manner, but for all time he is the model of that personage who is called The King." [8]

The key to the personal government of Louis XIV was a belief shared by the king himself, his ministers and courtiers, his official theorist Bishop Jacques Bénigne Bossuet (1627–1704), and by virtually all the people of France —the belief that all power and authority within the realm should emanate from the person of the monarch, who was himself unlimited and responsible to no one save God, in short, "sovereign." Inspired by this belief, and carrying on the work that had been begun so auspiciously by Richelieu, Louis set out systematically to destroy any possible source of opposition to his royal will. In staffing his government, he was not content simply to employ people on the basis of merit alone (the famous "career open to talents" of a later age), but rather he deliberately discriminated

[8] E. Lavisse, *Histoire de France* (Paris, 1906), vol. VII, pt. i, p. 138.

against the nobility and the great clergy, preferring always to elevate men of low degree who would thus be completely the creatures of his will. The institution of extraordinary courts, such as the famous Grands Jours d'Auvergne (1665 and after), provided striking proof that the king possessed both the determination and the power to discipline even the great nobility, a class which previously had been almost completely exempt from the rigors of royal justice. The effective implementation of royal policy was ensured by the employment throughout the length and breadth of the kingdom of thousands of royal administrative agents (*intendants* and their subordinates) whose sole loyalty was to the monarch and his state. The pretensions of the papacy in this Catholic state were vigorously denied in a Declaration of the Clergy of France issued in March 1682, the so-called Gallican Articles: "We accordingly declare that kings and sovereigns are subjected by the ordinance of God to no ecclesiastical power in temporal things." Thus for the first time in history a national state was effectively subjected to the will of a single man. Established at Versailles, where all the functions of government had been centralized, Louis XIV was indeed the Sun King around whose person revolved all the lesser figures of the political universe, warmed and illuminated by his reflected glory. Like James I of England, Louis believed himself the very image of God on earth; so compelling was his performance that it has been argued that to the seventeenth-century imagination God was a sort of image of Louis XIV! [9]

True to his original resolution, Louis apportioned the execution of his commands among several persons, scrupu-

[9] H. Taine, *La Fontaine et ses fables* (Paris, 1861), pp. 217–218; cited by Lavisse, *op. cit.*, p. 133.

lously retaining intact his own prerogative. Even the greatest of his ministers, Jean Baptiste Colbert (1619–1683), was vividly aware of the power of the Sun King's will: "Never as long as you live," Colbert wrote to his son and successor, "send out anything in the king's name without his express approval." The actual machinery of the central government remained essentially unchanged in form, although the role which the king chose to play altered its substance completely:

By a carefully calculated strategem the older institutions were deprived of their functions or transformed into new orders with old names. Whatever was vital or useful in the old system tended to be absorbed by a host of councils, bureaus, and ubiquitous officials divorced from all traditional allegiances except to the sovereign. These were the representatives and engineers of a regime of order and science, of the modern state in France.[10]

In short, the government of France was being bureaucratized as well as centralized; in place of the great noble personages of the past, the chief ministers of state were becoming professional, one might almost say "scientific," civil servants. Meanwhile, the entire governmental machine remained utterly subservient to the royal will. Clearly no individual, even one who possessed the prodigious energy of Louis XIV, could conceivably operate this machine singlehanded. Louis was able to achieve his goal of "governing" France largely because he possessed an extraordinary ability to discern and utilize the talents of others. Ever jealous of his own powers, he was nevertheless served by a suc-

[10] James E. King, *Science and Rationalism in the Government of Louis XIV* (Baltimore, 1949), p. 313.

cession of able advisers, whom he carefully played off against one another; any public servant who showed signs of overreaching himself was instantly dismissed, as was the case with Nicolas Fouquet, who had hoped to become Louis XIV's Mazarin and ended his life in prison. As might be expected, the men who rose to positions of eminence and power in this government were men who shared the monarch's passion for hard work and selfless devotion to the state, notably Colbert and Louvois.

Jean Baptiste Colbert stands as the perfect symbol of the modern state as it developed in France during the seventeenth century. Born in Reims, a member of a *petit bourgeois* family, he first tried his hand at business and banking and then entered the public service under Michel Le Tellier, the secretary of state for war. Mazarin soon recognized his extraordinary financial talents and made Colbert the administrator of his immense personal fortune. Shortly after the dismissal of Fouquet (1661), Colbert was made controller general of finance, a post which he retained until his death in 1683; in addition, he became superintendent of building and manufactures (1664) and secretary of the navy (1666) and of the king's household (1669). Under his tireless attention the entire economic life of France was organized to serve the interests of the state. Detailed standards for all branches of manufacture were issued and rigidly enforced; "infant industries" were established, freed from guild restrictions, and protected by tariffs; enterprises which were considered important to the state were granted special privileges, such as monopolies, and were financed at public expense to the extent of ten million *livres*; [11]

[11] The entire income of the government in 1626 has been estimated at eighteen million *livres*.

internal communications by land and water were vastly improved; a great navy was created to protect French commerce abroad; finally, the entire administrative and fiscal apparatus which had been inherited from Richelieu was ruthlessly reorganized and rationalized. The super-bureaucrat Colbert, obsessed as he was with a passion for routine and organization, was unquestionably the supreme practitioner of the doctrine of mercantilism. On the economic foundation which he had so painstakingly built rested the military establishment which had been created by his greatest rival, Louvois.

The marquis de Louvois (François Michel Le Tellier), Louis XIV's minister of war for the quarter-century between 1666 and his death in 1691, was not a "self-made man" in the sense that Colbert was—his father, Michel Le Tellier, had preceded him as minister of war—but he was even more of a career public servant; from the age of fifteen he had been carefully trained to fill his future position. Possessing many of Colbert's qualities, notably his zeal for order and efficiency and his capacity for hard work, Louvois created in France the first great modern army, numbering even in time of peace well over 100,000 men, and at its height 400,000. Led by the greatest general of the age, the vicomte de Turenne, and boasting the services of the marquis de Vauban and Du Metz, masters respectively of the sciences of fortification and artillery, this army was a fitting instrument to serve the will of the Sun King. More important than either its size or the brilliance of its leaders, however, was the fact—directly attributable to Louvois—that the French army was efficiently equipped and supplied, strictly disciplined (the name of General Martinet stands even today as a symbol of drill), and completely responsive to the will of the monarch as no army had ever been. Typical of the problems which confronted Louvois in his systematization of the French military establishment was the persistence of the tradition of selling commissions to members of great families; and equally typical was Louvois' solution: unable to do away with the practice altogether, he restricted it to colonels' and captains' commissions, and to each of these officers he attached a thoroughly disciplined and trained deputy—this is the origin of the ranks of lieutenant-colonel and lieutenant. Through the combined efforts of Colbert and Louvois, as well as those of many lesser figures, Louis XIV found himself master of the greatest and most effective military machine the world had ever known. We shall have occasion to examine the extravagant use to which he put it.[12]

The tragedy of the last years of Louis' reign—the longest in recorded history—must to some extent be attributed to the deaths in 1683 of Colbert and Maria Theresa, the queen, removing as they did the last effective voices of moderation and leaving the king more than ever open to the influence of Louvois. But much more important, indeed decisive, was the personality of the king. A man of overweening ambition, intoxicated with the visions of glory conjured up for him by Louvois, the Sun King illustrated to perfection that "restless search for power after power unto death" which we have noted as a characteristic of his age. Paradoxically, it was the very successes of Richelieu, Mazarin, and Colbert that set the stage for the transformation of Louis' government from an absolute monarchy to a despotism. In his domestic policy, Louis XIV was reminiscent of the soldier who "conquered every enemy that came

[12] See below, Chapter VII.

within his sight, and looked around for more when he was through." It is quite obvious that the wars of Louis XIV were made possible by the prior pacification and consolidation of his kingdom; in a sense, the same may be said of the most tragic and ill-advised act of his career—the revocation of the Edict of Nantes (1685). The Protestant community of France, which remained distinctly separate from the predominantly Catholic population and which tended to exhibit superior talents in commerce, industry, and finance, had in 1598 been guaranteed freedom to worship as they wished. Since the time of Richelieu they had clearly ceased to constitute a threat to the political unity of the kingdom, and during the wars of the Fronde they had actually supported the monarchy. Thus it cannot be argued that Louis' decision to revoke the Edict, literally outlawing Protestantism in France, was dictated by political necessity. Nor, in view of the king's espousal of "reason of state" and his general indifference to religious questions *per se,* can it be contended that the revocation reflected his desire to achieve doctrinal purity within his kingdom. It is true that a Catholic party at court, led by Madame de Maintenon, Louis' last mistress and secret wife, had urged this step. But infinitely more revealing were the terms of their appeal; they relied not on the king's regard for the safety of his kingdom or the souls of his subjects, but rather on his vanity. It was, they told him, an insult to his dignity that a million of his subjects should presume to hold themselves aloof from his faith and his church. And the Sun King was convinced. In the sequel, the decision to revoke the Edict of Nantes proved a disastrous mistake—over 200,000 Protestants fled the kingdom, a loss of talent and wealth which the nation could hardly afford—but it was a mistake completely in character. Quite literally, Louis found it necessary to do something, to find some challenge sufficient to stimulate his imagination, some enterprise worthy of his power and majesty. As the years passed, he pursued his grandoise international schemes with monomaniacal fury, making intolerable demands on the people of France and revealing that the Achilles' heel of Louvois' army was, as is so often the case, the treasury which supported it. When, in 1715, Louis XIV died, he left his people impoverished, his kingdom surrounded by enemies who thirsted for revenge, and his government in the hands of his sickly, five-year-old great-grandson. In the long run, the magnificent façade which he had reared was seen to be considerably more impressive than the structure which it covered.

CHAPTER VI

England: Constitutional Power⁓

THE achievements of Richelieu and Louis XIV made the triumph of the modern state secure on the continent by converting France into an autocratic monarchy. Its authoritarianism and its nationalism were given almost unlimited sway in the realm of His Most Christian Majesty. But the fulfillment of the modern state, and in a certain sense its conquest, were provided by constitutionalism, with its restraining of all authority by law, and by the division of governmental powers by a constitution. This vital achievement of the modern west, without which the flowering of science, technology, industry, and agriculture in the last two hundred years is inconceivable, was fought for and in its essentials largely accomplished by the people of England during the fateful century from the accession of James I (1603) to the accession of Queen Anne (1702). Marked by a great civil war and a bloodless "revolution," the execution of a king, and the short-lived attempt to establish a republican government, this dramatic era was crucial in the development of western civilization. For if the government that finally emerged from the British constitutional crisis was superficially less impressive than the magnificent Grand Monarchy, it provided in the long run the most satisfactory

solution to the problems raised by the great Leviathan, the
modern state.

Like the Thirty Years' War, the English civil war (1642–
1648) was in a very real sense a war of religion, precipitated
by the inadequacy of the old political institutions in resolv-
ing the tensions created by religious passion. Constitutional,
economic, and social factors played their roles, of course,
but they were all animated and, as it were, brought to
incandescence by the heat which the religious fire gen-
erated. Nowhere was the intimate relation between religion
and politics more clearly apparent than in seventeenth-century England, nor was the explosive potential of this relation more strikingly demonstrated than in the English civil
wars.

On the one extreme, there remained in England a small
but fanatical Roman Catholic minority, subject to varying
degrees of persecution as circumstances and the whim of
the monarch dictated, but always firm in their rejection of
the work of the Reformation. Since the English Reformation had to a unique degree been an act of state, it left
behind it a national church, the Church of England, of
unprecedented strength. Largely Protestant in dogma, the
Anglican church was a curious blend of Lutheran, Calvinist,
and Roman Catholic elements. It was characterized by a
strictly hierarchical, episcopal organization much like that
of the Church of Rome, save for the crucial fact that its
head was not the pope but rather the king. The mutual
dependence of church and monarchy was clear to all, and
not least to James I, whose epigram "No bishop, no king"
expresses the relation perfectly. But if James was aware of
his dependence on the episcopal Church of England, so
were the enemies of that church aware of its dependence

on the monarchy. Thus the more extreme Protestants—from the relatively conservative Presbyterians to the radical sectarians and Independents—found that their religious objective—the destruction of episcopacy and the substitution of a less rigid form of church government—inevitably involved political consequences. In practice the two extremes tended to meet, as the political position of these Puritans came to approximate that of their bitterest religious foes, the Roman Catholics; both denied the religious supremacy of the king, both accepted the view that "Christ Jesus is the King of the Church whose subject King James is, and of whose kingdom he is not a king, nor a lord, nor a head, but a member"—although the Catholics, of course, added a provision for Christ's Vicar on earth. This fact, too, James recognized. His bitter observation that "Jesuits are nothing but Puritan-Papists," while theologically bizarre, was politically quite sound. The story of the Puritans' struggle to vindicate their religious principles against the absolutist pretensions of the early Stuart kings is at the same time the story of the constitutionalizing of the modern state, for the Puritans were quick to assert the fact that they were also Englishmen and, as such, entitled to enjoy the already hallowed rights of Englishmen.

The Early Stuarts

James VI of Scotland, son of Mary Stuart and great-great-grandson of Henry VII, succeeded Queen Elizabeth on the English throne, as James I, in the year 1603. A man of whom it has been said that one could love or despise but not hate him, James I had good qualities such as learning, tolerance, and a measure of good will bordering on weakness, which helped him little to govern well, while he also had bad ones which made his ideas on government ineffectual pedantries: his vanity, his stubbornness, above all his lack of judgment of men and measures. James was no fool, but he inclined to overcleverness, and the contrast between what he conceived to be a king's right and position and what he was willing to do to live up to such pretensions bordered in its irresponsibility upon levity. As a result James, who liked to speak of himself as the "establisher of perpetual peace in Church and Commonwealth," precipitated the great controversies which wrecked the Stuart monarchy.

The pattern of this unhappy reign may be stated quite simply: by his divine-right doctrine James challenged the English parliamentary tradition; this tradition, intrinsically no more weighty than similar traditions elsewhere, gradually merged after 1610 with the political outlook of the Puritans' religious faith; and, as if this dual ideological mixture were not explosive enough, James reinforced it with economic self-interest by his arbitrary money-raising schemes; out of such a convergence of religious, legal, and economic frustrations the revolutionary impasse arose. In this particular age, the age of power through faith and of faith through power, the religious ingredient was probably the most important; certainly those who were strong in the Puritan faith took the lead in resistance to the royal pretensions.

The actual events of James's reign need not detain us long. Beset by rising expenditures which left an annual deficit of about £100,000, the king could neither rule without Parliament nor get along with it. His vacillating and weak foreign policy, inspired by the incompetent and unpopular duke of Buckingham (1592–1628), and particularly his unsuccessful attempt to negotiate a marriage between his son and the Spanish princess (lasting from 1611 to its ultimate failure in 1624), fanned the flames of parliamentary opposition. But even without these specific grievances, cooperation was clearly impossible between a king who believed that "as to dispute what God may do is blasphemy . . . so it is seditious in subjects to dispute what a king may do in the height of his power" and a House of Commons which declared (May 1610), "We hold it an ancient, general and undoubted right of Parliament to debate freely all matters which do properly concern the subject and his right or state." The inevitable climax was reached in 1621, when a petition of the Commons against popery and the Spanish marriage and the king's scathing reply ("bring stools for these ambassadors") elicited the Great Protestation (December) restating Parliament's claim to deal with "the arduous and urgent affairs concerning king, state, and defense of the realm." With characteristic vehemence and lack of insight, James tore the offending page from the Commons' journal, dissolved Parliament, and imprisoned its leaders. This sort of behavior, although perfectly suited to the rising absolutism of the age, had no place in English politics, as James's son was to discover.

The heritage which James I had left to his son, who as Charles I succeeded him in 1625, was not a cheering one. The treasury was perpetually empty, English prestige abroad had been brought to a low ebb by isolation and vacillation, and tempers in the country were irritable because of James's steady extension of the royal prerogative. Like his father, the young king was deeply imbued with the sense of a king's divine calling, and this inspired sentiment was fed by his deep religiosity. In feeling thus, Charles merely reflected a mood prevailing throughout Europe. From what he had seen in Spain during his ill-fated courtship and what he knew of France and the rest of the continent, he perceived a general sentiment supporting the sanctity of kings as the personification of communities no longer held together by a common religion. What he failed to sense were the unique and distinctive elements of the situation in England, where national feeling had already progressed to the point where it could take the place of religion. The consolidation of the English nation had arrived at the point where national representatives had become meaningful and conscious of their mission. This crucial fact—or, rather, the failure of Charles I to recognize this fact—led to the civil wars and the destruction of the Stuart monarchy.

The inexorable movement of events toward a crisis is nowhere better illustrated than in the history of Charles I's third Parliament (1628-1629). At first, although these men were determined to resist the king's efforts to assume supremacy, they did not attempt to make the Parliament supreme without the king either. When Charles attempted to raise money without parliamentary sanction to support his far-flung and unsuccessful policy of foreign intervention, Parliament responded with the famous Petition of Right (1628), declaring that the royal prerogative—for this was the term under which absolutism's claims were advanced in England—was to be excluded from two basic spheres of the national life, an Englishman's person and his property. Under the leadership of Sir Edward Coke, John Selden, and others, the Commons was still anxious to maintain that balance between crown and Parliament which had been the traditional pattern of the polity throughout the Middle

Ages and which the Tudors had left formally intact. The Tudor monarchs had had the support of the middle classes in their work of national unification. That work having now been consummated and the nation unified, the middle classes forthwith demanded to be heard. By the spring of 1629, as the result of Charles's arbitrary acts, this demand had taken the form of a revolutionary claim to parliamentary supremacy, now for the first time taken in the modern sense to mean commons without lords or king. This is the meaning of the Three Resolutions passed by the Commons in March, resolutions declaring anyone an enemy of the commonwealth who either brought forward religious innovation along the lines of popism or Arminianism,[1] or advised the levying of duties without consent of Parliament, or paid such duties—declaring, in short, that anyone who sided with the king on these issues was a traitor to his country. Charles forthwith dissolved the Parliament and committed its leaders to the Tower, including the greatest, Sir John Eliot, who in 1632 died a martyr to constitutional freedom and puritanical Christianity.

The dissolution of Parliament set the stage for Charles's attempt to emulate the example of his brother-in-law, Louis XIII, who had governed France without the Estates-General since 1614. However, in England there was no Cardinal Richelieu to aid the king; instead he had Archbishop William Laud (1573–1645), a pedantic, though well-intentioned bureaucrat, in love with "order" and the formalities of ritual worship. The years (1629–1640) during which Charles, misapprehending the traditional English meaning of the concept of monarchy, made the fateful attempt to extend monarchical power to the point where he might become

[1] See above, Chapter III, p. 47.

an absolute monarch in the continental sense, appear drab in retrospect. The weird expedients to which the king was driven by financial necessity might conceivably have become, with time, "precedents" which commons acquiesced in, as had comparable innovations in earlier periods, had he not accompanied them with thoroughgoing efforts to "force the conscience" of the more ardent Puritan spirits by an elaborately detailed ritual and hierarchy. Inspired by Archbishop Laud, these efforts revealed an utter failure to understand the deep, personal glow of Puritan religiosity, which struggled for a direct relationship between each person and his God, without the intermediaries of ecclesiastical organization and ritual. Instead, religion, to Laud, was ritual and ritual demanded conformity. Thousands of Englishmen, repelled by Laud's ritualism and sacramentalism, chose to cross the Atlantic and found the great Puritan commonwealths of New England; the majority, whether from more or less courage, chose to remain in England and fight back through their representative institutions. The conflict between Laud and his Puritan adversaries was neither accidental nor easily avoidable. Once the problem which the Reformation raised of the church and its government had reached the point where it must, in England as elsewhere throughout western society, be decided one way or the other, the right to have the last word (i.e., "sovereignty") became decisive, decisive not only in the ordinary political sense, but desperately decisive in a spiritual sense, because it involved a man's soul and his salvation. Either the king or the people represented in Parliament had to have the last word. Seen from this perspective, the three great developments of the first half of the seventeenth century were all of one pattern: the same issue was fought over on the battlefields of Germany, France, and England, and it was settled in favor of the proposition that some one governmental authority must have the last word. Here, in this proposition, the modern state emerged.

The events which ended Charles I's eleven years of personal rule embodied perfectly the forces at play in England's mounting constitutional crisis. The first step was religious: the attempt of Laud to impose in Scotland an Anglican uniformity of doctrine and discipline. The angry resistance of the Scottish Presbyterians and Charles's utter failure to subdue them in the two Bishops' Wars (1639–1640) led to the Treaty of Ripon, in which the king conceded complete defeat, acknowledged the Scots' religious and political claims, and agreed to pay an indemnity. In order to finance these wars, and more especially in order to pay the indemnity, Charles was forced to call two parliaments, the Short Parliament (April–May 1640) and the Long Parliament (November 1640, and after). Thus what had begun as a religious controversy, and had then become a military conflict, was now translated into the constitutional sphere. The Long Parliament's first act was to order the arrest of the king's chief councilor, Thomas Wentworth, earl of Strafford (1593–1641). When he fell on his knees before the lords on November 11, 1640, the king's cause was lost. The Parliament then proceeded to push through and get Charles's consent to an act which provided for regular meetings of Parliament (the Triennial Act, February 1641) and a special act which prohibited altogether the dissolution of the Long Parliament. Having thus entrenched themselves and their majority, the Parliament's leaders, John Pym and John Hampden, went on to tear down the edifice of autocratic government which the

Tudor and Stuart kings had fashioned. The Court of Star
Chamber and that of High Commission were abolished on
July 5, the ship money tax on August 7, and ecclesiastical
innovations on September 1. But the most crucial issue
was undoubtedly that of church government; the so-called
Root and Branch Petition (December 1640: episcopal
church government shall "be abolished, with all its depend-
encies, roots and branches") proposed to tear down one of
the pillars of the English constitution. At first this radical
measure seemed unlikely to pass, but in December of 1641
the indignation stirred up by the massacre of several thousand Protestants in Ireland made it possible for Pym and
Hampden and their followers to push through the Grand
Remonstrance. This document, which gained a majority of
twelve votes after what has been called the most bitterly
fought and most momentous argument in the history of the
English Parliament, included the essential features of the
Root and Branch Petition; in large measure, it was an appeal
to the people of England against the alleged usurpations
of the king. The two central demands of the Remonstrance,
the elimination of prelates from Parliament and the sharing
by Parliament in the choice of ministers, the king rejected
on the ground of the existing constitution. The Grand
Remonstrance was in effect, and presumably in intention,
an ultimatum. The king's proclamations rejected the ultimatum. War was bound to follow.

The Great Rebellion

The actual course of the English civil war need not concern us here. It is usually divided into two distinct wars,
the first lasting from the battle of Edgehill in October 1642
to the surrender of the king to the Scots in May 1646,

and the second from May to August 1648. After the initial military advantages of the royalists, called Cavaliers, had been played out, the balance slowly shifted to the parliamentary side, whose soldiers were scornfully called Roundheads. This shift was basically the result of the success of Oliver Cromwell (1599–1658) in building a semiprofessional army, the famous Ironsides, victorious in the decisive battles of Marston Moor (July 2, 1644), Naseby (June 14, 1645), and Preston (August 17–20, 1648). Like Gustavus II Adolphus some twelve years earlier, Cromwell concluded that the spirit of troops—what is nowadays called morale—was of crucial importance. The hard spiritual core of the Ironsides provided a foundation for a conception of duty to serve, which contrasted vividly with the personal bond of feudal loyalty. The contrast was even greater, of course, when the motive for enlisting in the king's forces was the fear of the impressed or the greed of the hired mercenary. The Protestant (and more especially Calvinist) idea that one's calling was the testing ground for divine favor found vigorous expression in the Ironsides' indomitable spirit. It is striking to read again and again, in the strictly military and practical reports of Cromwell, such sentiments as this: "Sir, this is none other but the hand of God; and to him alone belongs the glory, wherein none are to share with him." The modern historian may be excused for assigning a share of the glory to the military and organizational genius of Oliver Cromwell.

Considerably more important in the long run than the military course of the war was the sharp conflict which soon arose within the parliamentary camp between Presbyterians and Independents. Although this conflict did not prevent the final victory of the parliamentarians, it did determine the course of English politics for the next decade. True to the pattern by which revolutions characteristically move from the less to the more radical position, the Independents slowly extended their influence in the army, which offered them an opportunity to work for the cause in which they believed; meanwhile, the Presbyterians remained in control of the Long Parliament. After the surrender of Charles I (May 5, 1646), a bitter controversy arose between the majority in the New Model Army and the majority in Parliament. The first group desired genuine liberty of conscience and separation of all churches from the government, which many thought should be republican; the latter was prepared to set up a Calvinist church government and discipline under parliamentary control and supervision. These issues had been brewing ever since Cromwell first perceived the morale-building potential of the ardent religious feeling of the sectaries; it now flared forth in the form of intense debates within the army and a sharp conflict between the army and Parliament.

The radicalism of the army majority found its most striking expression in the Agreement of the People (October 1647), essentially the work of the revolutionary group who became known as the Levelers. This document contained the outline of a constitution for a republican commonwealth, conceived in terms of protecting the individual citizen against the arbitrary acts of the majority—the fundamental idea of modern constitutionalism. The very fact that the army was here taking the lead politically was itself revolutionary. When the king and Parliament, shocked and frightened by the temper of the army, decided to compose their differences, the army seized the king and proceeded to try him for high treason, after having (through

Pride's Purge, December 6, 1648) succeeded in subjecting the Parliament to its dominance. Unimpressed by Charles's claim that he had taken up arms "only to defend the fundamental laws of this kingdom," the specially constituted high court of justice adjudged that "he, the said Charles Stuart, as a tyrant, traitor, murderer, and public enemy to the good people of this nation, shall be put to death by the severing of his head from his body." This sentence was executed on January 30, 1649.

The Commonwealth and the Protectorate

After the death of the king two authorities remained in England: the purged remnant (or "Rump") of the Long Parliament, dominated by the Independents and clothed in the last tattered shreds of legitimacy, and the victorious New Model Army, led by Oliver Cromwell and possessing a clear preponderance of force. In assessing the subsequent actions of these two bodies, it is vital to keep in mind the fact that, with the exception of the Levelers on one extreme and the Presbyterians on the other, the antimonarchical forces in the civil wars had fought for constitutionalism, not for democracy, for the rule of law, not for majority rule, for a man's right to a free conscience, unrestrained by ecclesiastical regimentation, not for his right to vote and elect. Thus the great, the everlasting struggle of Oliver Cromwell throughout the succeeding years was to find a constitutional legitimacy, not a popular majority.

The core of the revolutionary position was clearly revealed in the second Agreement of the People (January 20, 1649), which the council of officers of the New Model Army presented to the Rump Parliament; it recommended a government of elected representatives under a constitution protecting freedom of religion and conscience. As Cromwell had foreseen, the Rump declined to act upon the army's urgent recommendation. But on May 19, 1649, it did declare England to be a Commonwealth, after having appointed a council of state and abolished the office of king and the House of Lords.

Meanwhile, the son of Charles I set about energetically to reconquer his lost dominions. When the Scots joined forces with the self-styled Charles II, Cromwell vainly attempted to persuade them that they were betraying their own cause: "I beseech you, in the bowels of Christ, think it possible you may be mistaken." When the Scots refused to see the light, he set out to crush them militarily; his brilliant victories at Dunbar (September 3, 1650) and Worcester (September 3, 1651) made the king-pretender a fugitive and eliminated the last danger of foreign invasion. But was the Commonwealth to be free? Had the people been able to elect responsible representatives in accordance with their preferences? Unfortunately Cromwell's striking victories in the field yielded no such issue. Indeed, the necessity for these military exertions turned the Commonwealth into the path of dictatorship, from which it found itself unable to turn for its duration.

The crucial issue of constitutionalizing the revolutionary power was the election of a new Parliament. When, after eighteen months of temporizing, the Rump still refused to yield to Cromwell's demands that it dissolve, Cromwell could contain himself no longer. On the fateful day of April 20, 1653, when the House of Commons was approaching a vote on a new election law, he strode into the house and cried out, "You are no parliament, I say you are no parliament; I will put an end to your sitting: call them in, call them in!" At this order two files of musketeers marched in and cleared the chamber. The Commonwealth was at an end; although true in fact for some time, it was now apparent to all that the Commonwealth had turned into a military dictatorship. The next five years were filled with Cromwell's efforts to mend the breach he had created and to establish by deliberate effort a constitution which would perpetuate forever the commonwealth of the "Saints."

A military dictatorship which sought to constitutionalize itself in the face of a hostile general public—that was the paradox of Cromwell's Protectorate. Somehow the Lord failed his "Saints" by not enlightening the majority of Englishmen about the benefits to be derived from their rule. Theoretically, Cromwell and his army officers would have liked to secure popular support by general elections, which was clearly the only basis of legitimacy which their general outlook implied. Unfortunately, as they knew only too well, the majority of Englishmen were either indifferent, disaffected, or increasingly inclined to return to the old constitutional order. Hence, the only way out was a restrictive electoral system, which in due course produced the subservient "nominated" Parliament (July–December 1653). Despite the purity of its intentions, this body proved utterly incapable of transacting practical business and soon humbly returned its commission to the actual master of the situation, Oliver Cromwell. Immediately upon the Parliament's resignation, the army came forward with an Instrument of Government, which after some debate Cromwell accepted.

The Instrument of Government provided that Oliver Cromwell was to become Lord Protector of the Commonwealth of England, Scotland, and Ireland and was to share the supreme legislative power with an elected, triennial parliament, and the executive power with a council of from thirteen to twenty-one members. He was to conduct foreign affairs, except for the declaration of war and peace, which was to require the consent of the council; and he was to exercise emergency powers with a similar consent. Parliamentary consent was required in all matters of legislation and taxation, and no adjournment or dissolution was permitted during the first five months of parliamentary sittings. The Protector's office, while for life, remained elective. Detailed provisions were laid down for electoral representation, and a £200 qualification for voters was specified. In addition, the Instrument included strongly worded articles protecting freedom of religion (excepting popery and prelacy!). It has been said, and rightly, that the Instrument of Government was the first fully elaborated modern constitution, based upon the division and balance of governmental authority and upon the recognition of at least one fundamental right. In this highly creative age, the Instrument of Government ranks with Rembrandt's paintings and Descartes' philosophy among the greatest works of superlative and lasting value. Begotten by the bitter experience of despotism of either monarch or representative, the Instrument sought a balance as the basis of a permanent settlement; its greatest weakness was the lack of support of either tradition or popular enthusiasm.

The next five years amply demonstrated how serious this weakness was. In the face of continuing parliamentary attempts to change the Instrument of Government, and pressed by the demands of his popular war against Spain (1656–1659), Cromwell came increasingly to rely upon the emergency administration of his major-generals—officials who, through their Puritan rigor, their arbitrariness, and their financial exactions, became thoroughly hated throughout the country. At the same time Cromwell remained unable to secure a solid backing for his broad conception of tolerance; the Anglicans and Presbyterians on the one hand, and his own narrowly Puritan army on the other, would not hear of it. So eventually the Lord Protector found himself alone, inspired and inspiring, but unable to stabilize a liberal order. Behind a façade of power and glory, Cromwell's dictatorship was being undermined by the same corrosive forces which seem inevitably to attack such regimes. On September 3, 1658—the anniversary of his victories at Dunbar and Worcester—Oliver Cromwell died, an intensely human being and a true embodiment of that practical idealism which represents the genius of his people. The Protectorate did not long survive its creator.

There is little of interest in the rapid disintegration of a rule which could not have been perpetuated even by its architect and master. Within a few months Richard Cromwell, who had succeeded his father as Lord Protector, was "Tumbledown Dick," and the generals who took over began quarreling among themselves. George Monk (1608–1669, later duke of Albemarle), one of Cromwell's most able and level-headed generals, cut short the developing chaos. Throwing in his lot with the civilians, he called for a parliamentary election, and the people's representatives called back Charles II. A restoration of the historical constitution was the line of least resistance; Englishmen were tired of innovation. Yet in a sense this very restoration reaffirmed the value of constitutionalism—a key tenet of the Puritan opposition to Charles I's government of church and state. It was a lasting achievement. The enduring inheritance of England's revolution has been this lesson in the importance of organizing a government according to and under a basic law, with powers divided and defined. Strikingly reasserted in 1688, it was the fulfillment of the emerging modern state.

The Restored Monarchy

When Charles II entered London on May 29, 1660, amidst the delighted acclaim of his people, he is said to have remarked to one of his companions, "I never knew that I was so popular in England." The spirit of comedy was to succeed the heroic tragedy of Cromwellian dictatorship as the English people joyfully turned their backs on a decade of puritanical repression; in a last outburst of vengeful fury, a London mob dug up Cromwell's bones and strung them to a gallows. But if the Restoration proved anything, it was that the tide of history cannot be turned back, that the work of a great revolution, no matter how hateful it may seem in retrospect, cannot be undone. The government which was "restored" in 1660 was, in fact, not precisely the same as any that had existed before; but it was certainly much closer to the parliamentary monarchy of the Long Parliament than to the personal rule which the first two Stuarts had endeavored to establish. This was strikingly demonstrated when the Convention Parliament (April–December 1660), which had invited Charles II to return to England, declared valid all acts of the Long Parliament which had received his father's assent, including those which had abolished the prerogative courts.

The carefree spirit that greeted the return of Charles II was destined to be short-lived. Once the initial sense of release and exhilaration had worn off, it became clear that many of the old problems remained. The religious divisions, for instance, were as deep as ever, and the dangers inherent in this fact were not mitigated by the king's sincere desire to establish religious toleration. Indeed, the king's efforts on behalf of liberty of conscience were a source of constant friction between the crown and the overwhelmingly Anglican Cavalier Parliament (1661–1679). Throughout its long life this parliament fought a running battle with Charles II in an attempt to discriminate against both Roman Catholics and those Protestants who refused to subscribe completely to the Anglican Book of Common Prayer, the so-called Nonconformists. The opening salvo in this battle was the Clarendon Code, a series of four repressive measures passed by the Parliament between 1661 and 1665: the Corporation Act (1661) provided that all magistrates should take the sacrament according to the usage of the Church of England; the Act of Uniformity (1662) required all clergymen, college fellows, and schoolmasters to accept without reservation the Book of Common Prayer; the Conventicle Act (1664) forbade Nonconformist religious meetings; the Five Mile Act (1665) required all who had not subscribed to the Act of Uniformity to take an oath of nonresistance, swearing never to attempt any change in church or state, and forbade any Nonconformist clergyman to live or visit within five miles of any town where he had acted as minister. The chief consequence of this code was social rather than religious; from this time forth the Anglicans constituted a privileged group within the country, while Nonconformists were driven in increasing numbers into trade and commerce. Not until the mid-nineteenth century did the Nonconformists receive full equality and cease to form a distinct body of interest and opinion in England.

The Clarendon Code had been directed primarily against nonconformity and was clearly motivated by the Anglicans' desire for revenge for the indignities which they had suffered at the hands of the Puritans during the interregnum. Soon, however, the religious problem took a new form, as Roman Catholicism became the *bête noire* of Parliament and people alike. Complex as it is, the story of anti-Catholicism is essential to an understanding of the troubled years between the Restoration and the Glorious Revolution of 1688. Two facts are clear: in May of 1670 Charles II signed a secret agreement with Louis XIV (part of the Treaty of Dover) promising that at the first possible moment he would join the Church of Rome and make England a Catholic commonwealth; furthermore, Charles's younger brother James, the duke of York and heir apparent to the throne, made no secret of the fact that he was a Catholic. From this time forth Parliament waged an unrelenting struggle against Catholicism in general and the succession of the duke of York in particular. The men who passed the Test Act in 1673 (compelling all public servants to take the sacrament of the Church of England) and the Papists' Disabling Act in 1678 (excluding Roman Catholics from Parliament), the men who were terrified and enraged by the "Popish Plot" (1678) invented by the unsavory Titus Oates, the men who twice sought to enact a bill excluding the duke of York from the succession, were motivated by more than a simple abhorrence of the Roman Catholic faith. Although the secret terms of the Treaty of Dover had not yet been revealed, these men were united in their fear of three things which they believed to be intimately connected: Catholicism, France, and arbitrary royal power. Out of their determination to oppose this threatening alliance grew what was to become the Whig party, led by the earl of Shaftesbury (Anthony Ashley Cooper, 1621–1683) and inspired by the political philosophy of Shaftesbury's physician, John Locke.

In order to understand the growth of this opposition party within the Parliament, it is necessary to look more closely at the devious and remarkably successful intrigues carried on by Charles II. Although not a man of strong principles, Charles was motivated by an unceasing desire to increase the power of the crown to a point where it would be independent of parliamentary control; he chose as his model his cousin, Louis XIV. Despite the similarity of their goals, Charles II differed from his father in two crucial respects: he was an infinitely more skillful politician, perhaps because of his very lack of principles, and he had lived through both the civil wars and eleven years of exile. This last was an experience which Charles could not forget; when at the end of his reign he had substantially achieved the power which he sought, he used it with considerable moderation because, as he admitted, he was resolved "not to go on his travels again." But this resolution, so symbolic of the achievement of the Great Rebellion, did not destroy the king's determination to enhance his power; rather it simply dictated his use of more devious means. Instead of openly defying his parliaments, Charles II used two other methods: he first discovered a way of becoming independent of them, and he then began to practice the art of manipulating them.

As we have seen, the problem of finance had frustrated the attempts of the early Stuart kings to rule without Parliament. Now, in the person of Louis XIV, Charles II found an unfailing source of money. The prolonged col-

laboration between the king of England and the *Roi Soleil*
is one of the most bizarre episodes in English history, and
at the same time one of the most striking illustrations of the
workings of monarchical "reason of state." Louis, who at
this time was embarking on his most aggressive foreign
policy,[2] desired English neutrality and was frightened by
the growing anti-French sentiment of the English Parliament. Charles, who had no particular interest in a war with
France, wished to become financially independent of his
Parliament. This coincidence of interests expressed itself in
a series of secret agreements by which, between 1670 and
1681, the French king doled out hundreds of thousands of
pounds to his English cousin, on condition that Charles
either dissolve or suspend (prorogue) his parliaments! Thus,
for example, an agreement in 1675 provided that if Parliament were to appropriate money for a war against France,
Charles would dissolve it and receive instead £100,000 a
year from Louis. The results of this collaboration were eminently satisfactory on both sides: Britain and France remained at peace until after the overthrow of the Stuarts in
1688, and Charles II had succeeded, by the end of his reign,
in raising the power of the crown to heights unseen since
the time of the Tudors.

French gold, however, is not in itself sufficient to account
for the successes of Charles II. One must not overlook his
own political skill and the fact that throughout his reign he
was served by a succession of extraordinarily able advisers.
The particular talents of Charles's advisers illustrate very
well the development of the monarchy during this period.
The first of these men, the earl of Clarendon (Edward
Hyde, 1609–1674; lord chancellor 1660–1667) was ideally

[2] See below, Chapter VII, pp. 175 ff.

suited to the task of re-establishing the monarchy in England, having devoted his life to the service of law, constitutionalism, and the ideal of monarchical legitimacy. The dismissal of Clarendon in 1667, although nominally a victory for Parliament, actually served to strengthen the hand of the king. Whereas the lord chancellor had symbolized constitutionalism and the rule of law, he was succeeded by a group of ministers who were truly the king's servants, the Cabal—so called because of the initials of its members (Clifford, Ashley, Buckingham, Arlington, and Lauderdale). In this council composed of the chief officers of state, some historians have detected the beginning of the cabinet system; be that as it may, the Cabal served briefly as an effective instrument of the royal will. Perhaps more significant in the long run was the career of Charles II's last great minister, the earl of Danby (Thomas Osborne, 1631–1712; lord treasurer 1673–1679). Making skillful use of the money available to the crown, Danby was a master of the art of parliamentary management and has been called the inventor of the political "machine"; the immediate origins of the Tory party are to be found in the members of Parliament whose support he bought for the king.

The last years of Charles's reign (from about 1681 to 1685) were marked by the king's successful attempt to discredit the Whigs and to undermine the power of Parliament and of the independent municipal corporations. By giving the headstrong Whigs enough rope to hang themselves, by purchasing seats in Parliament, and by revoking municipal charters, Charles II ensured the victory of the Tory reaction; his political astuteness and his willingness to sacrifice principle to expediency had raised the power of the crown to new heights. But when, in 1685, his brother

James succeeded him on the throne, a constitutional crisis was virtually guaranteed. For James II (1633–1701), in his stubbornness and unwillingness to compromise, was much more reminiscent of his father than of his brother. An open and devout Roman Catholic, he was determined to undo the work of the last century and to establish for his coreligionists not only equality but political dominance. Thus, once again, it was religion that revealed the fundamental ambiguities of the English constitution and led to a final resolution of these ambiguities in the settlement of 1689.

The pro-Catholic activities of James II had hardly begun (with the well-deserved punishment of Titus Oates in May 1685) when there occurred an event which strengthened his position just enough to allow him to destroy himself. In June 1685 the duke of Monmouth (1649–1685), an illegitimate son of Charles II, landed in southwestern England with a small army and proclaimed himself king. This quixotic expedition, known as Monmouth's Rebellion, was easily stopped by the forces of James II; but it provided the king with an excuse for a frontal attack on his enemies and allowed him to build up a considerable pro-Catholic army. Immediately after Monmouth's execution, Lord Jeffreys, James's chief justice, was sent on a circuit in the west to try the rebels. This he did with unparalleled brutality. To the great anger of the Protestant population of England, upon his return from these "Bloody Assizes," Jeffreys was forthwith made lord chancellor. During the next two years James and Jeffreys systematically set about to destroy the body of anti-Catholic legislation that had been built up during the last reign. In 1687 seven bishops, including William Sancroft, the archbishop of Canterbury, were thrown into the Tower for refusing to read in their churches the king's declaration of liberty of conscience—a declaration which they regarded as illegal. Law after law was broken by the king, as the royal prerogative was carried to lengths never before seen in England. The turning point, however, came on June 10, 1688, when a son was born to James II. Prior to this date, a majority of Tories had stood with the king despite their abhorrence of his religion; to them the preservation of the monarchy was all important. Now, after the birth of an heir to the throne, it became apparent to the Tories that the monarchy they were defending was destined to be a Catholic monarchy even after the death of James II. This prospect was unthinkable, and for the first time Protestant opinion—Whig and Tory alike—was united against the king. The acquittal of the seven bishops (June 30, 1688), greeted with an outburst of popular enthusiasm, signaled the beginning of the Glorious Revolution.

The Glorious Revolution and After

Although the Tories' desertion of James II made the Glorious Revolution possible, the revolution itself—which, in fact, was not a revolution at all—represented the final triumph of the Whig principles of constitutionalism and limited monarchy. The events of 1688–1689 may conveniently be divided into two parts: (1) the successful invasion of England by William of Orange and James II's flight to France and (2) the Revolution Settlement which established William and Mary as constitutional monarchs. Immediately after the acquittal of the seven bishops, an invitation was sent by "seven eminent persons" to William of Orange, the husband of James II's daughter Mary, asking him to save England from Catholic tyranny. Eager to bring

England into the war against Louis XIV [3] and impressed by the stature of the men who had signed the invitation (the dukes of Devonshire and Shrewsbury, the earl of Danby, Lord Lumley, Henry Sidney, Admiral Russell, and the bishop of London, Henry Compton), William set sail from Holland with an army of 14,000 men. Driven back by a gale on his first attempt, William was soon favored by the famous "Protestant wind" and landed at Torbay on November 5, 1688; the banner under which he marched bore the traditional motto of the House of Orange, "I will maintain," to which had been added the words, "the liberties of England and the Protestant religion." As a result largely of the fifth-column work of William's commander, Lord Churchill (1650–1722; later duke of Marlborough), the army of James II melted away, while men of every class and party flocked to Exeter to pledge their support to William. Even now, James II could almost certainly have retained his throne had he been willing to call a parliament and submit to its will; instead he escaped to France (December 22, 1688), where Louis XIV established him at the Court of St. Germain. An irregular Convention Parliament was summoned by the peers of England on January 22, 1689, and six days later it declared:

That King James the Second, having endeavored to subvert the Constitution of the Kingdom, by breaking the Original Contract between King and people, and by the advice of Jesuits and other wicked persons having violated the fundamental laws and withdrawn himself out of the Kingdom, hath abdicated the government and that the throne is thereby vacant.

The phrase about James's "abdication" was inserted at the insistence of the diehard Tories, but it is quite clear that the Whig theory of contract and constitutionalism had won

[3] See below, Chapter VII.

the day. The arbitrariness of James II, combined with his Catholicism, had revealed to the people of England the dangers inherent in the all-powerful modern state; having deposed their king, they were united in their determination to subject this state to the rule of law. This is the enduring significance of the Revolution Settlement.

The throne being vacant, the immediate task was to fill it—not on any terms, but rather on the conditions laid down by the Convention Parliament in its momentous Declaration of Rights (February 13, 1689; subsequently confirmed by the parliamentary Bill of Rights, December 16, 1689). On February 23, 1689, William of Orange and Mary, his wife, jointly accepted Parliament's offer of the throne, and with it the provisions of the Declaration of Rights. This declaration, which in effect constituted an "original contract between King and people," was in form a reaffirmation of those "true, ancient and indubitable rights of the people of this realm," which had been violated by James II and which the new monarchs swore to uphold. These rights are so crucial to any constitutional system, and so central to the British form of government, that we may be forgiven for enumerating the most important of them: (1) making or suspending any law without the consent of Parliament is illegal, (2) levying money without consent of Parliament is illegal, (3) the maintenance of a standing army without the consent of Parliament is illegal, (4) it is lawful to petition the sovereign, (5) it is lawful for citizens to keep arms, (6) elections of members of Parliament must be free, (7) there must be freedom of debate in Parliament, (8) excessive bail should never be demanded, (9) juries should be empaneled in every trial, and (10) Parliament should meet frequently.

Although some of its provisions were new, such as the

prohibition of a standing army in time of peace, the Declaration of Rights was in essence a conservative document, a defense of the British constitution and of the rights of Englishmen, occasioned by the autocracy of James II. The people of England and their representatives in Parliament were determined that the nature of this constitution and of these rights should once and for all be made explicit. Thus, although the details remained to be worked out during the succeeding centuries, the years immediately following the accession of William and Mary saw the creation of a system of government based on the rule of law and the supremacy of Parliament. In one of his first executive acts, William III guaranteed the independence of the judiciary by appointing judges for the duration of their good behavior, as determined by Parliament, rather than at the will of the king. The Mutiny Act (1689) ensured Parliamentary control of the armed forces by making military discipline dependent upon an annually passed statute. The Toleration Act (1689) granted to Protestant dissenters the right of free public worship (but not civil and political equality). The Triennial Act (1694) guaranteed the regular meetings of Parliament, and the expiration of the Licensing Act (in 1694) signaled the end of censorship of the press. The work of this most conservative of revolutions was completed by the Act of Settlement (June 1701). In addition to providing for the succession to the English throne—and thus ensuring the peaceful change from the Stuarts to the house of Hanover on the death of Queen Anne in 1714—this act specified that all future rulers of England should be members of the Anglican church and should agree not to involve the country in a foreign war without parliamentary consent. Taken together, these acts constitute the so-called

Revolution Settlement—the creation of the most important modern national constitutional state. A distinguished historian of the Glorious Revolution has written:

Long use and custom have made liberty and peaceful self-government natural to Englishmen, and therefore they still survive the dangers of our own time. It is because the House of Commons has always governed the country since 1689, that it is able to govern us still, when popular assemblies of later birth have had their brief day and disappeared. It is because Englishmen two and a half centuries ago were set free to worship, to speak and to write as they pleased, that they are free still while so many others have lost their less ancient liberties.[4]

The most striking feature of the government that emerged from the Revolution Settlement was not its constitutionalism, however. In its essence, this issue had been settled much earlier in the century; what remained to be seen was whether a constitutional government could also be a workable and efficient government. In other words, could a system that by definition involved division and limitation of power, and the subjection of such power to law, hope to rival the monolithic efficiency of the absolute monarchy that reached its peak in the rule of Louis XIV? The events of the reign of William III answered this question in the affirmative. William was a strong king and a constant user of the royal prerogative, but he retained throughout his reign the support of the people and of their representatives in the House of Commons. The House of Commons, secure in its own power and for the first time in a century unafraid of royal pretensions to absolutism, co-operated with the

[4] G. M. Trevelyan, *The English Revolution 1688–1689* (London, 1938), pp. 201–202.

crown in the pursuit of a vigorous and successful foreign policy. Having finally settled her constitutional crisis, England could now afford the luxury of a strong executive. The state of mind that lay behind the Whigs' support of William was perhaps best expressed by John Locke in his chapter "Of Prerogative":

Where the legislative and executive power are in distinct hands (as they are in all moderated monarchies and well-framed governments) there the good of society requires that several things should be left to the discretion of him that has the executive power. For the legislators not being able to foresee and provide by laws for all that may be useful to the community, the executor of the laws, having the power in his hands, has by the common law of nature a right to use it for the common good of society. . . .[5]

Just as the earlier conflict between king and Parliament had been characterized by the Commons' continuing reluctance to grant money to the crown, so now the resolution of this conflict was symbolized by the creation in England of the first truly effective and modern fiscal system. Based on the proposition that the king's ministers were responsible to Parliament for their actions, and taking advantage of popular confidence to establish the first regular national debt, this system was productive of revenue as none had ever been before. The wars that bankrupted the Grand Monarchy of Louis XIV were easily financed by the treasury and the newly created Bank of England (1694). The English experience was to prove that, in the long run, the power of an executive who rules by common consent and with the confidence and support of his people is greater and more enduring than that of the most impressive autocrat.

[5] Locke, *op. cit.*, ch. xiv, p. 80.

In the course of the seventeenth century the people of England had succeeded in taming the great Leviathan, the modern state; they had not destroyed its vast might, but rather had made it responsive to their will and subservient to their law.

CHAPTER VII

Toward a New Balance of Power

THE distinguished historian, Professor G. N. Clark, has calculated that during the entire seventeenth century there were only seven complete years in which there was no war between European states: 1610, 1669–1671 and 1680–1682. Furthermore, when wars occurred—as they did with such depressing regularity—they were seldom fought out between just two contestants, but rather they tended to involve great alliance systems embracing many powers. As a consequence, many of the leading powers of Europe were actively engaged in warfare for more than half of the century, while for the other states, diplomatic negotiation and military preparedness were an urgent and ever-present necessity. In short, as Clark points out, war "may be said to have been as much a normal state of European life as peace." Shocking as this statement may be—and it is perhaps less so in our own time than it would have been during the two intervening centuries—it raises important questions for the historian. Most obviously, it raises the question, Why were there so many wars during this period? One might be tempted to dismiss the extraordinarily belligerent record of the seventeenth century with the observation that it was simply a natural consequence of baroque man's fascination with power. But to do this would be to ignore the fact that these men fought for something more than sheer, undifferentiated "power"; rather, they fought for certain specific objectives, objectives which were meaningful only within the given political context. Thus, although it may be true that their ultimate motivation was the "restless desire of Power, after Power, that ceaseth only in Death," the historian must concern himself with the particular forms which this desire took.

Certain far-reaching general developments and broad patterns are discernible within the field of international politics in the seventeenth century; it is to these that we must turn before examining in any detail the relations among the states of Europe. Perhaps most striking of all, in terms of the great sweep of European history, was the decline of Spain. Formerly the most powerful nation in Europe as well as the leader in the colonization of the non-European world, Spain during the seventeenth century fell to a position of minor—but not negligible—importance among the great powers. Although the process of decline had begun in the sixteenth century and was to continue through the eighteenth, its influence was most deeply felt during this period. If one accepts the notion of "power vacuums," lacunae which must somehow be filled, it is easy to view the meteoric rise of France as a corollary of Spanish weakness; on the other hand, it may also be argued that the spectacular successes of France were a contributing cause of the weakness of Spain. Be that as it may, the fact remains that under Richelieu, Mazarin, and especially Louis XIV, the French monarchy achieved a position of unquestioned supremacy on the continent. Alliance after alliance was formed with the explicit purpose of containing the expansive force of the Grand Monarchy, and some of these alliances achieved considerable success; but their very existence serves to dramatize the crucial importance of France's role in the international politics of the age of power. By default of the Spanish, the task of opposing French designs on the continent fell primarily to the two leading commercial powers of the age, England and the Netherlands. Despite the fact that both were Protestant countries, their conflicting mercantile interests led them often to open hostility. Finally, however, under William III they were united to form a bulwark against the aggressive designs of Louis XIV. From this time forward England was a factor to be reckoned with in the politics of the continent, pursuing with remarkable consistency and success a policy designed to maintain the European balance of power. In central and eastern Europe, too, revolutionary changes were occurring. Following upon the virtual disappearance of the Holy Roman Empire as a significant factor in international politics, Prussian and Russia rose to the position of great powers under the guidance of two extraordinarily able leaders, the elector Frederick William of Brandenburg (1620–1688) and the tsar Peter I (1672–1725). In the second half of the seventeenth century these two new powers came to dominate the area around the Baltic Sea, displacing Sweden, Denmark, and Poland. Finally, the success of the Austrian Hapsburgs in stemming the westward expansion of the Turkish Empire laid the foundations for their future hegemony in the southeast.

Even this bare outline suggests certain conclusions about the pattern of international politics in the seventeenth century. In the first place, it is clear that religion played a constantly diminishing role in the relations among nations during this period. It is noteworthy, for instance, that the papacy, which had formerly been such a potent participant in affairs of state throughout Europe, had virtually nothing to do with the developments which we have traced. Similarly, religious allegiances and controversies, which had been at the very heart of the Thirty Years' War, played an exceedingly minor role in the complex international drama of the later seventeenth century. It is customary to describe this change by saying that the age of religious wars had ended and that it was replaced by the age of power politics. In a sense, this is a perfectly true and accurate statement. It is perhaps more useful, however, to say that the successor to the age of religious wars was the age of "reason of state." For the crucial fact is that the participants in the international relations of the later seventeenth century—the dramatis personae in this vast European drama —were neither religious sects nor royal dynasties, but rather secular, territorial states, the products, at least in part, of the political genius of such figures as Richelieu, Wallenstein, and Gustavus II Adolphus. In their tradition, the objectives for which these new states fought and negotiated were defined—albeit not always overtly—in terms of their secular interests, or "reasons of state." Thus, in a very real sense, it may be argued that the history of international politics in the seventeenth century is the story of the creation of the modern European state system. Furthermore, it should be noted that the word European is used here deliberately. In this period—for the first time—the area stretching from Russia and Turkey on the east to England on the west, from Scandinavia on the north to the Iberian peninsula on the south, became truly a political unit, in the sense that the nations included in it acted within a common frame of reference and were aware always of the interrelations of their actions. True, one may still speak of "the Baltic powers" and even of "the Balkan question," but it is clear that these subsidiary issues were precisely that —subordinate parts of what contemporaries, with their baroque sense of the dramatic, were pleased to call "the theater of Europe."

Before looking more closely at the process which led to the creation of this European state system, we must pause briefly to introduce two of its most important participants, men whom history has deemed worthy of the epithet "great": the Great Elector of Brandenburg-Prussia and Peter the Great of Russia. In the careers of these men one may observe with unparalleled clarity the deliberate, conscious attempt to erect a modern state, and one may observe also the vital relationship between domestic and foreign politics in this age of power.

The Great Elector

The House of Hohenzollern, electors of Brandenburg, inherited the fief of Prussia in 1618, when the male line of the dukes of Prussia died out. Nine years earlier the Hohenzollerns had established their claims on the Rhine as a part of the disputed Jülich succession. Thus the east-west span of their dominions was laid out, which during the next two hundred years would be rounded out and eventually expanded into the German empire that collapsed in 1918. But during the generation immediately following these acquisitions, Brandenburg-Prussia played a largely passive role under the direction of her weak prince, George William (1619–1640). No sooner had Frederick William, his gifted son, ascended the throne than the situation began to change.

The young prince, though only twenty years of age, displayed a remarkable sagacity in his dealings with an all but hopeless situation—"a beggar on horseback," his most recent biographer has called him.[1] Although his extended dominions consisted largely of claims, he proposed to maintain these claims with the utmost vigor.

He decided to make haste slowly. Trained in the Netherlands, he would doubtless have liked to work in close cooperation with the House of Orange, and in 1646 he married the daughter of the prince of Orange, Louise Henriette. But the failure of the Dutch merchant republic to become his ally (they saw him only as an impoverished prince), turned the elector's eyes back to the east. He had gained much in the Peace of Westphalia,[2] but the gains did not include all of Pomerania, which he considered his rightful inheritance. A generation had to pass before he could seize through war what peace had denied him.

In the meantime he faced another perplexing problem. He held Prussia as a fief of Poland. The Polish king, Ladislas VII (1595–1648), although a weak ruler, insisted upon the formalities, and the proud young prince was obliged to proceed to Warsaw to render homage to his liege lord. He did so in 1641, enduring this spectacular event as a crushing humiliation. With the passing of time, his bitterness increased until an attack on Poland in 1655 by the brilliant young Swedish king, Charles X Gustavus (1622–1660), presented him with an opportunity for escape from this humiliating dependence.

By that time Frederick William had come to the conclusion that he must provide himself with a standing army.

---

[1] Ferdinand Schevill, *The Great Elector* (Chicago, 1947), ch. iii.
[2] See above, p. 95.

His experiments with temporary forces, like the ones he had raised in 1644 and in 1651 in his abortive attempt to force the issue of his claims in the west, had shown him that such forces made him dependent upon the estates of his various dominions, a dependence which threatened disaster. When the clash between Sweden and Poland seemed imminent, therefore, he established the nucleus of a permanent organization to defend himself and his territories against his two more powerful neighbors. The year 1655 may properly be designated as the birth year of the Prussian army, an army which in the course of time became the symbol of militarism and aggression. In the beginning, however, the new force was clearly defensive. As he told the Prussian estates in 1662, the great elector had come to recognize that "the conservation of his state and country would depend next to God upon arms"; a few years later in his testament to his son he added that "alliances are good, but one's own forces are even better."

It was Frederick William's determination to create a standing army, a *miles perpetuus,* as the times called it, which lay at the heart of his protracted struggle with his estates, a situation similar to that in France a generation earlier. But whereas in France the estates were completely eliminated, in the Hohenzollern realm they remained functioning elements of the government throughout the Great Elector's reign and later. Their effectiveness, however, was reduced by their rigid insistence upon local patriotism. Thus there were separate estates in Prussia and Brandenburg, in Cleve-Mark and in Pomerania, as well as in the lesser component units of the Great Elector's dominions. In each of the three larger units, Brandenburg, Cleve-Mark, and Prussia, a long-drawn-out controversy between Frederick William and the estates over whether the prince could permanently maintain an armed force ended with the victory of the elector. The perils of the war between Sweden and Poland, combined with the renascent aggressiveness of France after 1660, convinced the more recalcitrant representatives of the "people" of the cogency of the monarch's argument. To meet a permanent threat there must be a permanent security force—an argument familiar again in our time. Nor should it be forgotten that, in fact, the provincial estates represented only the feudal landlords, now on the way to becoming agricultural capitalists, and the burgher element of the towns, but not the peasants and more dependent workers. Indeed, in 1653 Frederick William was forced to concede to the Brandenburg estates a reaffirmation of the right of the feudal lords to hold the peasants in virtual serfdom, and ten years later the same right was confirmed in Prussia (March 1663).

In contrast to his persistent, though occasionally frustrated, attempts to establish absolutism, greeted by many as tyranny that should be resisted, Frederick William's policies proved singularly enlightened in the field of religion. Although an ardent Calvinist himself, he insisted upon the basic similarity of the two Protestant faiths and generally pursued with unrelenting vigor a policy of broadminded tolerance, a policy which reached its climax in the Edict of Potsdam (November 1685), issued in response to Louis XIV's revocation of the Edict of Nantes. There is something Cromwellian in the character of Frederick William, which combined religious piety, administrative skill, military ambition, and broad tolerance with occasional outbursts of rage when he encountered bigotry, disloyalty, or wanton opposition.

The consolidation of Frederick William's dispersed possessions into a single modern state advanced slowly, and it was severely strained by the war between Sweden and Poland which Charles X Gustavus precipitated in 1655. We may trace briefly the means by which the elector exploited the varying fortunes of this war to wrest advantage for himself by a series of "treaties" culminating in that of Oliva (1660). His chief problem arose from the fact that in this war the unavowed aim of Sweden was the conquest of Prussia; control of the Prussian coast would nearly complete Swedish control of the shores of the Baltic and make that sea a Swedish lake. Realizing this fact, Frederick William had attempted, in spite of his bond to the Polish king, to negotiate with Sweden beforehand. When the haughtiness of the Swedes frustrated this attempt, the elector could rely only upon a treaty of mutual defense with the Dutch, in which he secured their naval protection for his Prussian ports in exchange for granting them maintenance of existing tariff rates.

The startling and overwhelming initial victories of Charles X, as a result of which the whole of Poland lay prostrate at his feet within a few weeks, forced the elector to accept the terms of the Treaty of Königsberg, acknowledging the suzerainty of Sweden over Prussia, opening the ports of Memel and Pillau to Sweden, and granting the Swedes a share of their customs (January 1656). When, as a result of an outburst of Polish national resistance, Charles X began to meet with reverses, the elector found himself in the happy position of being wooed by both sides. Since the Poles had little to offer but risks, the elector concluded another treaty with Sweden, at Marienburg (June 1656), in which he gained large parts of western Poland between Prussia and Brandenburg in exchange for armed support to Charles X. By this time Frederick William had assembled a well-organized Prussian army of about 8,500 men; they won their spurs in the great battle of Warsaw (July 1656), in which the Poles were badly beaten.

This proved a Pyrrhic victory for Charles, for it brought Austria and Denmark into the fray and forced him to turn west to meet the new threat. Meanwhile, the elector returned to Prussia, after repeatedly (but vainly) urging his ally to conclude peace. Determined to crush Poland, Charles soon renewed the attack, but not before he was obliged to grant Prussia its sovereign independence and to relinquish the Swedish share in the customs of the Prussian ports in the Treaty of Labiau (November 1656). While Charles was occupied in the west, the elector proceeded to open negotiations with Poland and its allies, as a result of which the Polish king recognized the sovereignty of Prussia in return for Frederick's promise to abandon all claims to Polish territory outside the duchy that had been promised him by Sweden.

In spite of the startling successes scored by Charles X against Denmark which culminated in the Danish surrender at Copenhagen (1659), the Swedes finally quit, and the Treaty of Oliva (1660) concluded the Swedish-Polish war which had threatened to engulf Brandenburg. Due to his statesmanlike skill and moderation, Frederick William gained from this war not only international recognition as sovereign of the Prussian duchy, but also greatly enhanced prestige both at home and abroad. The Treaty of Oliva marked the turning of the tide against Sweden's Baltic empire and the emergence of Brandenburg-Prussia as the effective rival of Sweden and Poland for predominance in northeast Europe. The elector's swift maneuvering has been both denounced as an immoral disregard of all rules of good faith, and celebrated as a sign of true greatness. In fact it was neither. It was the ruler's steady and sober pursuit of his state's interests in the approved and prevailing fashion of the baroque age. The failure of Brandenburg to gain at least a part of Swedish Pomerania by the terms of the Treaty of Oliva provoked the elector's later international exploits. He was now a European sovereign in his own right, and his remaining task—namely, to link the scattered areas of the Hohenzollern domains—became the concern of this rising dynasty for the next two hundred years.

During the first two decades of his reign the Great Elector had been preoccupied with foreign concerns; his chief domestic interest during these troubled years, as we have seen, had been the creation of a disciplined, reliable standing army. Now, after the Treaty of Oliva, he was free to turn to the problem of the internal organization of his domains. Without losing sight of immediate military and diplomatic necessities—his army grew constantly to a maximum size of 40,000 men in 1678—Frederick William undertook during these years the task of constructing a powerful, unified state. If power was his ultimate goal, he realized that domestic prosperity and order were the means to its achievement. In the mid-eighteenth century the French philosopher Jean Jacques Rousseau wrote that an infallible sign of good government is a growing population. Although his reasoning was quite different from Rousseau's, the Great Elector seems to have shared this view. Throughout his reign he actively encouraged immigration into his domains, and he was particularly anxious to foster the colonization of the sparsely settled areas of Brandenburg and East

Prussia. In this connection, his avowed policy of religious toleration became highly useful to the interests of the state; Lutherans and Calvinists alike, fleeing persecution elsewhere, were welcomed by Frederick William and remained to contribute to the prosperity and strength of Brandenburg-Prussia. Particularly important was the influx of nearly 150,000 Huguenots, who settled in Brandenburg after the revocation of the Edict of Nantes, in direct response to the elector's invitation embodied in the Edict of Potsdam. Combining this population policy with the familiar techniques of mercantilism—the improvement of communications and the encouragement of industry and agriculture through the instrumentalities of the state— Frederick William succeeded in laying the foundations upon which the future greatness of Brandenburg-Prussia was built.

More than any other European ruler, the Great Elector may be said to have created a state as a deliberate, conscious act of will. Although quantitatively his achievement can hardly be compared with that of Louis XIV, in one respect it is even more impressive. The very fact that Louis was king of France implied, inevitably, that he would be a figure of immense importance on the European scene; he might have been more or less ambitious, and more or less successful, but history guaranteed him a place in the sun, simply because he was head of the House of Bourbon and ruler of a great power. The situation was quite different for Frederick William. The House of Hohenzollern was simply one among many minor German dynasties. Its possessions were relatively small and widely scattered, and its claim even to these was disputed. In the harsh world of seventeenth-century diplomacy, a world in which "the big fish devour the little fish by natural right," a ruler of average talents might well have congratulated himself for maintaining intact his tenuous hold on these domains. But Frederick William was by no means a ruler of average talents, nor was his goal the modest one of survival. Fired by an insatiable desire for power and glory—which has led his biographer to state that "Brandenburg's outstanding baroque exhibit was the Great Elector himself"—he succeeded in the course of sixty years in turning his unpromising inheritance into a major European power. While history and tradition dictated the greatness of the monarchy of Louis XIV, the Great Elector willfully carved out his own destiny and that of his state.

Peter the Great

In the year 1613 Russia emerged from its anarchic "time of troubles." A national assembly (the *zemski sobor*) elected to the throne Michael Romanov, the grand-nephew of Ivan the Terrible, and for the next seventy years Russia was ruled by Michael, by his son Alexis, and by his grandson Feodor III. In contrast to the anarchy of an earlier age, or to the absolutist monarchical regime of the tsars after 1689, this may be called the brief oligarchic period of Russian government. Among the most notable events of the period must be reckoned the new code of laws passed by the *zemski sobor* in 1648–1649 and formally attributed to Tsar Alexis, a code which remained the basis of Russian law until 1832. Its aristocratic flavor is revealed by the fact that it finally riveted serfdom upon Russian society as a legal institution. The development of serfdom—which converted a free peasantry into a species of slaves who were tied to the soil on penalty of death and exposed to cruel

extortions and brutal treatment generation after generation
—was the most disastrous and most important event of this
period.

Broadly speaking, the pattern of the age was one of reconstruction, as the tsardom received the support of the
most influential elements of the population, and notably of
the so-called "service gentry," who realized that such
support was the only means of preventing a return to the
anarchy of the early seventeenth century. There were two
notable exceptions which did not support the tsar: the religious group known as the Old Believers and the peasants
of southeastern Russia. As their name indicates, the Old
Believers were a profoundly conservative group; they objected strenuously both to the religious reforms undertaken
by the patriarch Nikon (1605–1681) and to the general
westernizing tendencies of the government. Although they
were condemned by a church council in 1667, the tradi-
tionalist, nationalist beliefs which motivated them have
continued to this day as a powerful force in Russian life.

The second major source of unrest during the reigns of
the first three Romanov tsars was a great peasant revolt,
led by the Don Cossaks, under Stenka Razin (d. 1671), in
the years 1670–1671. This revolt was finally crushed, but
only after a long, difficult, and bloody struggle. By the end
of the reign of Alexis, however, the position of the central
government had been firmly established, despite the fact
that its foundation was exceedingly narrow even when
measured by the standards of the seventeenth century.
When Feodor III died in 1682, he was succeeded by his
feeble-minded brother Ivan and his half-brother Peter,
while their sister Sophia acted as regent. Seven years later,
in 1689, Peter overthrew the regency and established him-

self as sole ruler of Russia, a fitting beginning for one of the most extraordinary reigns in modern history.

Physically a giant, a man of great intelligence and unbounded determination, completely ruthless but also completely dedicated to his country and his people, Peter I occupies a position in the history of Russia similar to that of the Tudor monarchs in England, Louis XIV in France, and Frederick William in Prussia. In short, he stands as the creator of the modern Russian state. One historian describes his role:

Up to his time the political sense of the people had, as regards public life, identified the State idea solely with the person of the Tsar . . . but these two conceptions Peter separated by legalising separate oaths of allegiance both to the Tsar and to the State, and insisting that the supreme and unconditional norm of any State system was the State's interest, even though that might involve the Sovereign himself, for all that he was the State's paramount dispenser of law, the public weal's paramount overseer, playing second fiddle to that interest. Peter, therefore, considered his every act a personal service to the State.[3]

This conception of service, which so strikingly anticipates Frederick the Great's proud dictum, "I am the first servant of my state," [4] is the key to the understanding of the reign of Peter the Great. Indeed, like those of Louis XIV and the Great Elector, Peter's achievement suggests that only a monarch inspired by such an ideal is capable of eliciting a similar response from his subjects and thus of building a great state.

Throughout the thirty-six years of his reign, Peter's foremost concern was to strengthen the international position

[3] V. O. Kluchevsky, *A History of Russia* (New York: E. P. Dutton & Co.; London: J. M. Dent & Sons, 1926), IV, 217.

[4] See Manuel, *op. cit.*

of Russia, to win for her the status of a great European power. Although he is equally famous for his policies of domestic reform—for establishing the power of the central government, for creating an effective bureaucracy, for rehabilitating the economy of his country—in each case the initial impulse was the tsar's military ambition, his desire to create a fighting force that could prevail over those of his great rivals, Sweden and Turkey. Never noted as a theorist, Peter was first led to reform and then impelled along this path by the exigencies of war; his policies were inspired more by urgent necessity than by any preconceived plan. In 1695 a Russian expedition which sought to win the fortress of Azov from the Turks, thus gaining access to the Black Sea, was resoundingly defeated. The young tsar was quick to learn the lesson of the relation between internal organization and military capacity; after months of careful and arduous preparation, Azov was taken in 1696. This early experience set the pattern for the remainder of Peter's reign. Every defeat was taken as evidence of the need for further reform, and even victories became the occasion for redoubled effort. Thus, after his great triumph over the Swedish army at Poltava (July 1709), the tsar wrote a brief *History of the Swedish War*, which he began by remarking that this success should not be permitted to interfere with the vital work of domestic reconstruction upon which depended the enjoyment of the advantages won at Poltava.

By far the most spectacular manifestation of Peter's passion for reform and modernization was his journey to western Europe in the years 1696–1698, the first such journey ever made by a Russian tsar. He went not as a reigning monarch visiting his royal "cousins," but rather as a private citizen under the name of Peter Mikhailov; the official motto of the mission to which he attached himself was, "I am among the pupils, and seek those who can teach me." With considerable insight, Peter had concluded that the political and military successes of the states of western Europe were the fruit largely of their scientific and technical achievements; only by duplicating these achievements could Russia hope to meet her western rivals on their own terms. Thus, he believed that those who could teach him were above all the scientists and technicians, the shipbuilders and craftsmen, the bureaucrats and military experts of these states. After traveling through Germany, where he became a close friend of the elector of Brandenburg-Prussia, Peter settled in a humble cottage in the Dutch village of Zaandam and found work as a common shipwright. When his identity was discovered, he moved to Amsterdam, journeying thence in all directions to visit factories, shipyards, museums, hospitals, and other institutions in which the new technology of the west could be studied. By the time of his return to Russia, after visiting and studying in London and Vienna, Peter had recruited more than a thousand technicians for the imperial service and had himself become a highly skilled naval architect and shipwright. It was symbolic of Peter's position that his travels in the west should have been cut short by an uprising of the conservative, aristocratically led palace guard, the *streltsi*. Clearly, the process of modernization could not succeed so long as the embittered remnants of the old order were able to frustrate the forces of the new. This threat to his program was met by Peter with characteristic ruthlessness and efficiency.

Returning to Russia in the early summer of 1698, Peter immediately determined to make a public example of the *streltsi* who had revolted during his absence. Since the ranks of the palace guard were filled with Old Believers, he recognized that this was an opportunity to strike out at all the major forces of conservative opposition within his realm, to crush aristocrats, Russian nationalists, and reactionary churchmen at one blow. As reported by the Austrian ambassador, Peter, with his own hands, tortured and killed the first five of the condemned rebels and required that each of his principal officials should personally kill a given number. About a thousand brutal executions followed as the full fury of the tsar became manifest. During the course of this blood bath Peter issued an edict which, although trivial at first sight, revealed the depth of his passion for westernization and modernization: he ordered that no one should enter his presence wearing a beard, he levied a tax on beards, and he personally shaved the beards of five of his lieutenants. At the same time, Peter took steps to outlaw the long robes which, like the beard, had been a part of traditional Russian garb. Discussing the tsar's motives, Kluchevsky has written:

He would attach the more importance to these trifles because of the impressions gathered during his boyhood, gathered during the period when trifles of the sort had figured exclusively on *streltsy* and Old Believers—on persons, that is to say, in rebellion against the State. Yes, that must have been the reason why he came so instinctively to view the old-established Russian beard as something beyond a mere physical feature of the masculine countenance, and to class it with the pristine long-skirted habit as a sign, as a mark, of a certain political attitude, of opposition to the State's authority.[5]

It is no exaggeration to say that Peter's ultimate aim was the alteration of the very ethos of the Russian people, the eradication of every vestige of their old way of life. Clearly,

[5] Kluchevsky, *op. cit.*, IV, 225.

such a transformation was beyond the power of any man; but it must be added that Peter the Great came perhaps as close to success as was humanly possible. His heroic efforts stirred Russian society to its depths and created tensions and conflicts that have not been resolved to this day.

The suppression of the *streltsi* was a vivid illustration of the negative aspect of the Petrine reforms; more important in the long run were the tsar's positive, constructive policies. Since Peter's model was always the west, these policies did not differ in substance from those of the great state-builders whose work we have already discussed. For this reason, and also because the period of the greatest reforms (roughly, 1715–1725) falls outside the scope of this book, it is not our intention to describe in detail the steps by which the political, economic, and military institutions of the modern state were created in Russia. Spurred on by the disastrous battle of Narva (November 1700), in which 40,000 Russian troops were crushed by 8,500 Swedes under his archenemy, Charles XII, Peter personally supervised the recruitment and training of an army of 100,000 men, rendered "immortal" by a regular system of conscription, as well as the building and outfitting of an effective fleet in the Baltic Sea. Recognizing that an extensive and efficient military establishment depends upon a smoothly functioning political bureaucracy and a fruitful revenue system, he first extemporized by carrying on with the numerous *prikazi* (bureaus) to handle the affairs of government and then regularized this system, first by the institution of a ten-man administrative senate and then by the creation of ministerial "colleges," modeled after those of Sweden, which had been recommended to him by Leibniz. Financial necessity, and specifically the need for increased revenue to support his military ventures, led to Peter's reform of the systems of taxation and municipal government. Elected officials, called *burmistri* after the burgomasters of Germany, were intended both to weaken the power of the traditional nobility and to improve the collection of taxes in their towns. Similar reforms in the church, in industry, and in every part of the life of Russia, considerably enhanced the power of the central government, which was the power of the tsar, to order the life of his subjects.

If the substance of Peter's reforms was essentially similar to that which emerged in the west during the seventeenth century, the manner in which these reforms were carried out was distinctively Russian. Impressive though they were, the autocracies of the west never approached the thoroughness, the rigor, or the ruthlessness of Peter's despotism. One example will suffice to illustrate this difference. It will be recalled that mercantilism was an integral part of the process of state-building in the west and that the deliberate fostering of native industries was a distinctive feature of mercantilism. The monarchs of the west, however, were generally content to establish a royal company, to manipulate tariffs to its advantage, to give it loans and perhaps tax exemptions, to grant it a monopoly, and to appoint officials to see that it maintained certain standards in its operation. Forced labor was rare. All of this Peter did too, and on a magnificent scale, but his unique position and his extraordinary character made it possible for him to do more. For example, he was able to provide the managers of his state enterprises with an unfailing supply of cheap labor simply by giving them absolute power over the lives of the peasants in their locality. Despising the luxury of a Versailles, the tsar traveled tirelessly through the provinces of his realm.

living when necessary in peasants' huts, supervising the work of his servants, and applying his great technical skills to improve their efficiency. In the words of a recent historian, "Peter was first of all a mechanician. His first toys were pieces of machinery. He not only shaved his courtiers' beards; he was his own court dentist and kept in a little bag the teeth which he had extracted; but the object to which he applied all his technical knowledge was the possession and extension of power." [6]

For Peter, as for his contemporaries in the west, power was measured above all by the standard of success or failure in the great arena of international politics. More specifically, Peter's goal of establishing Russia as a great European power involved wresting control of the Baltic from Sweden and access to the Black Sea from the Turks. The counterpoint between these two objectives characterizes the diplomacy and warfare of his reign. Briefly, Peter had inherited from his predecessors a war with Turkey. Having captured Azov in 1696, and having failed to gain western support for the continuation of this war, he concluded peace with the Turks in 1700, on terms which allowed Russia to retain Azov. On the very next day—August 18, 1700—Peter declared war against the Swedes under their able leader Charles XII, having first secured guarantees of support from Saxony and Denmark, later joined by Poland (1704). Undiscouraged by his initial defeat at Narva, Peter won one of the decisive battles of Russian history at Poltava in 1709, a victory which finally destroyed the power of Sweden in the north and guaranteed Russia's position as mistress of the Baltic.

[6] Sir Bernard Pares, *A History of Russia* (New York, 1946), p. 200.

The Great Northern War, as it was called, dragged on for twelve more years until, by the terms of the Treaty of Nystadt (1721), Russia gained Livonia, Estonia, Ingermanland, part of Karelia, and a number of Baltic islands. Meanwhile, after the victory of Poltava, the war with Turkey had been renewed, largely due to French diplomacy and the machinations of Charles XII, who had fled to Turkey. Peter's army of 40,000 men was surrounded by a vastly superior Turkish force on the River Pruth, and the tsar was fortunate to negotiate a treaty, the Treaty of Pruth (July 1711), which limited his losses to the surrender of Azov. Not until the reign of Catherine the Great was it to be recovered by Russia. In conclusion, then, it may be said that Peter succeeded in fulfilling half of his ambition; he had won mastery in the north but had been stalemated in the south. Actually, his achievement was infinitely greater than such a statement would suggest. With his "window on the west" in the Baltic, Peter had won the prize that he most desired. From that time down to the present day, Russia has been a force to reckon with in the councils of Europe. By a truly superhuman effort Peter the Great had, in fact, transformed his isolated, backward, disorderly land into a modern state and a great European power.

The Hapsburgs and the Ottoman Empire

Peter the Great was not the only European monarch of the seventeenth century whose ambitions brought him into conflict with the forces of the still powerful Ottoman Empire. During the entire latter half of our period the lands of southeastern Europe, known now as the Balkans, were the scene of almost unceasing wars, fought chiefly by the Austrian Hapsburgs and the Turks. The major arena of this conflict, as well as its chief prize, was Hungary, and particularly its eastern portion, the independent kingdom of Transylvania, of which the Hapsburgs were hereditary kings. In the course of time, however, what had begun as a local war fought for territorial objectives became increasingly entangled in the great European alliance systems of the age of Louis XIV and eventually culminated as the last of the crusades of Christendom against Islam. The story of these complex developments, a story which illustrates once again the growing unity of European politics, can only be sketched briefly here.

The policies of the Austrian Hapsburgs, and of their able and tenacious emperor Leopold I (1640–1705), were to a great extent dictated by geographical considerations. Located as they were in the very heart of Europe, the domains of the Austrian Hapsburgs, like the two-headed eagle of their crest, faced both east and west. As a result, the emperor was constantly, and understandably, concerned to avoid involvement in a war on two fronts, while his enemies, with equal logic, sought to maneuver him into precisely this position. More specifically, Austria's interests in Germany and the Netherlands made her look with fear upon the aggressive designs of Louis XIV, while at the same time her hereditary claims in Hungary were threatened by the policies of the vigorous Turkish viziers of the Kuprili family, who virtually ruled the country after 1656. During the years 1661–1664, while Louis was still occupied with the task of consolidating his power within his own realm, the Austrians and Turks fought an indecisive war, terminated by the twenty-year Truce of Vasvár. Despite the brilliant successes of his general, Count Montecuccoli,

Leopold accepted at Vasvár terms that included the surrender to Turkey of some Hungarian territory. The reason for this concession, characteristically, was Leopold's fear of prolonged involvement in the east in the face of the deteriorating international situation in the west. Angered by what they considered to be a betrayal at the hands of their putative defender, the nobles of Hungary looked first to France and then to Turkey for support against the emperor. Needless to say, both Louis XIV and the Kuprili viziers were delighted by this opportunity to foster revolt among the emperor's subjects.

By 1682, in spite of years of diplomatic efforts to prevent it, Leopold faced the very situation that he most feared. In the west, and notably in the Rhineland, Louis XIV had embarked upon the policies of aggrandizement that were to lead eventually to the War of the League of Augsburg.[7] In the east, Kara Mustafa (vizier from 1676 to 1683) had gathered a vast army of some 200,000 men and, at the urging of the French ambassador and the nobles of Hungary, was preparing to march up the valley of the Danube River toward Hungary and Austria. Hopelessly outnumbered, the imperial army under Charles of Lorraine fell back before the Turks, and on July 14, 1683, Kara Mustafa laid siege to the city of Vienna. For two months the population of the city held out despite frightful hardships; the heroic garrison under Rüdiger von Stahremberg repulsed the Turks time and again. Finally on September 12, just as the limit of their endurance had been reached, the citizens saw in the distance the vanguard of a great German-Polish relief army, led by Charles of Lorraine and John Sobieski (1624–

[7] See below, pp. 181–182.

1696), the king of Poland. After the high drama of the siege and the arrival of the army of liberation, the hasty withdrawal of the Turks came as a distinct anticlimax.

The siege of Vienna awakened Europe to the danger of the resurgent forces of Islam. Leopold concluded that the future of his state depended upon the final expulsion of the Turks from Hungary. If this were achieved, he reasoned, Austria could once more become a great power capable of opposing the designs of Louis XIV; if not, she would remain perpetually harried by threats from two directions and unable to meet either. Acting on this conviction, Leopold determined to make peace with France in order to have a free hand in the east. In August 1684 a truce was signed at Regensburg between the temporarily satiated Louis XIV and the Hapsburg rulers of Austria and of Spain. Meanwhile, the great Odescalchi pope, Innocent XI (1611–1689), had inspired (and financed) the formation of a Holy League dedicated to driving the Turks from Europe. Although the treaty that formed the League (March 1684) was couched in religious terms, it is quite clear that its chief members—Austria, Poland, and Venice—sought more mundane, territorial rewards. Conspicuous by his absence was Louis XIV, whose policies of "reason of state" had earned for him the not undeserved title of "the most Christian Turk of Versailles." The forces of the Holy League, swelled by volunteers from every country of Europe, pressed forward relentlessly, retaking Budapest (1685) and Belgrade (1688). Finally, in September 1697, with the end of the War of the League of Augsburg which had absorbed Austrian energies for almost ten years, Prince Eugene of Savoy (1663–1736) virtually annihilated the Turkish army in the great battle of Zenta. Although the war dragged on for several months thereafter, the might of the Ottoman Empire had been broken at Zenta. By the terms of the Treaty of Karlowitz (January 1699), Austria was granted all of Hungary, Transylvania, Croatia, and Slavonia; Venice and Poland too were handsomely repaid, at the expense of the Turks, for their participation in this great crusade. With the destruction of Turkish power in Europe, the focus of international politics turned once more to the west, to the France of Louis XIV.

The Wars of Louis XIV

The Thirty Years' War in Germany, the wars of the Fronde in France, and the English civil wars of 1642–1648 had signaled the emergence of the modern state as the characteristic political institution of western Europe. It was inevitable that such a truly revolutionary development in domestic politics should have far-reaching repercussions in the realm of international politics. On the one hand, as we have noted, the declining importance of dynastic and religious questions created a situation in which sheer power came increasingly to dominate the relations among states. On the other hand, the centralized bureaucratic institutions of the modern state placed in the hands of monarchs and parliaments alike new techniques—economic, diplomatic, and military—which were peculiarly appropriate to the pursuit of their states' interests in the international "war of all against all." Nowhere are these parallel forces more vividly illustrated than in the history of the reckless expansionism of Louis and the opposition which it aroused during the last fifty years of our period. Here, in the so-called "wars of Louis XIV," were established the basic patterns that have characterized international relations down to our own century.

The wars whose collective title stands as a fitting monument to the aggressive designs of the Sun King were four in number: the War of Devolution (1667–1668), concluded by the Treaty of Aix-la-Chapelle; the Dutch War (1672–1678), concluded by the Treaty of Nimwegen; [8] the War of the League of Augsburg (1688–1697), concluded by the Treaty of Ryswick; and, finally, the War of the Spanish Succession (1701–1714), concluded by the Peace of Utrecht and the Treaty of Rastadt and Baden. Together, these wars filled more than thirty of the fifty-five years of Louis' personal reign, bankrupting his kingdom and causing the deaths of hundreds of thousands of his subjects—in a single battle (Malplaquet in 1709) the French suffered more than 12,000 casualties. A generation brought up on socioeconomic or geopolitical explanations of the phenomenon of war may well view with suspicion any attempt to argue that these wars were in fact the direct consequence of the megalomania of a single man, urged on by an ambitious minister and by his own insatiable ambition. A brief examination of the wars themselves, and of the events leading to them, however, may perhaps provide evidence in support of just this argument.

The international position of France at the beginning of the period of Louis XIV's personal rule was defined by two recently concluded treatises: by the terms of the Peace of Westphalia (1648) her eastern frontier was established on the Rhine, a bastion against the alleged hostile designs of the Hapsburg emperor and (more realistically) a conven-

[8] Spelled also Nijmwegen, Nijmegen, and Nimeguen.

ient base for further operations in Germany; under the Treaty of the Pyrenees (1659) she received territories in the Spanish Netherlands, and, more important, she demonstrated her ascendancy over the Spanish Hapsburgs, symbolized by the marriage between Louis XIV and the eldest daughter of Philip IV, Maria Theresa. Thus, in 1661 the territories of France stretched from the Atlantic Ocean to the Rhine, from Flanders to the Pyrenees; rich in natural resources and with a population far exceeding that of her neighbors, she was the unquestioned mistress of western Europe. To contemporaries, and notably to her ruler, there seemed to be no limits to the greatness which she might achieve.

Louis' first opportunity for positive action came with the death of his wife's father, Philip IV of Spain, in 1665. Previously, his role in the Anglo-Dutch commercial war of 1665–1667—in which the British seized the city of New Amsterdam and renamed it New York—had been ambiguous in the extreme. Although bound to the Dutch by an alliance (1662), and actually providing them with troops, he concluded a secret treaty with Charles II of England in 1667, under which he promised to withold all naval assistance from the Dutch. The fact is that Louis was interested in this war only as a prelude to the fulfillment of his own designs in the Spanish Netherlands. It will be recalled that, upon her marriage to Louis XIV, Maria Theresa of Spain had renounced all claim to her Spanish inheritance, upon condition that Louis was to receive a dowry of 500,000 crowns from Spain. The dowry had never been paid, and now in 1665 Louis published his claim to all Spanish possessions in the Belgian provinces; this claim he justified in terms of a provision of private law known as the "right of devolution," by which the daughters of a first marriage had priority over the sons of a second. When the Spanish refused to accept his demands, Louis coolly proceeded with the military occupation of all the territories in question; by May of 1667, as a result of the skill of Turenne and the overwhelming superiority of the French armies, all of the Spanish Netherlands lay open to the Sun King. Confronted with so formidable a threat, the states of western Europe began, characteristically, to forget the differences that divided them. The war between the English and the Dutch was replaced by an alliance, which was soon joined by the Swedes—the Triple Alliance of 1668. Negotiations were at the same time begun between Spain and Portugal, with a view to freeing the Spanish for action against France. Louis' immediate response to the formidable coalition that was being formed against him was an attempt to conciliate the Dutch by turning his attention eastward. Having successfully occupied the Spanish territory of Franche-Comté, on the Swiss border, he then announced his willingness to negotiate a settlement of the war. By the terms of the Treaty of Aix-la-Chapelle (May 1668), he restored Franche-Comté to the Spanish but was allowed to retain twelve fortified towns in the Netherlands. The events of the brief, inconclusive War of Devolution are of particular interest for three reasons: (1) they represent the first of Louis XIV's attempts to extend the frontiers of France by any and all available means, legalistic, diplomatic, or military; (2) the Triple Alliance was the first instance of a combination of traditionally hostile European powers on the basis simply of their common fear of French power; (3) by ordering the destruction of all fortifications in Franche-Comté before returning it to Spain, by insisting on the

retention of fortresses in the Netherlands, and by concluding a secret treaty with the emperor Leopold for the future
division of Spanish territories (January 1668), Louis XIV
gave clear indication that he regarded the Treaty of Aix-
la-Chapelle as no more than a temporary truce. Thus, while
the War of Devolution was still in progress, the Sun King
was already laying his plans for the next war.

Quite apart from his continuing determination to win
the Spanish Netherlands, Louis was now motivated by a
profound hatred of the Dutch, who had frustrated his ambitions in 1668. He immediately set about to achieve the
diplomatic isolation of Holland, concluding treaties with
England (1670) [9] and Sweden (1672); as French gold was
used to buy English neutrality in the forthcoming war, so
too it was used to buy active German support in the cities
of Cologne and Münster. The years between 1668 and 1672
were years of preparation which Lionne, the secretary of
state, spent laboring with all his might to secure allies,
Colbert to find money, and Louvois to raise soldiers for
Louis. By May of 1672 the preparations were complete and
French armies were once more loosed upon the United
Provinces. Again they met with immediate and overwhelming success; only the opening of the dikes saved Amsterdam
from capture. In August an enraged mob murdered the
brothers John and Cornelius De Witt, leaders of the Dutch
aristocratic republican party; William III (1650–1702),
prince of the House of Orange, the future king of England,
took over the leadership of the United Provinces and in
time became the chief organizer of European resistance to
France. Almost immediately the fortunes of the Dutch
improved; alliances with the Great Elector, with the em-

[9] The secret Treaty of Dover; see above, page 138.

peror, and with Spain ended their position of diplomatic and military isolation, so carefully created by Louis XIV. As the French squandered their initial advantage through their passion for siege warfare, the conquest of the Netherlands became an ever more remote possibility. Once again, Louis' eyes turned toward the east: he personally led the force that recaptured Franche-Comté, while Turenne waged a campaign of stunning brilliance in the Palatinate and along the upper Rhine. For years the war dragged on, marked by stiffening opposition—diplomatic and military —to the designs of France. Finally, in 1678 and 1679, a series of treaties among the participants brought the war to a close. The results of the Franco-Dutch War were strikingly similar to those of the War of Devolution: once again Louis had failed to win the Spanish Netherlands; once again his actions had stimulated the formation of an anti-French coalition, this time under the extremely able leadership of William of Orange; and once again his chief gains were on France's eastern border, this time including Franche-Comté. Although largely unseen by the participants, a continuing pattern was beginning to emerge in the relations among the states of western Europe.

The Treaty of Nimwegen is often said to mark the zenith of the power of Louis XIV and the nadir of that of his enemies. This being the case, it is clear that even at the height of his success the Sun King was unable to achieve the objects of his ambition, while from this time forward his fortunes could only decline. Like most men of overweening pride and ambition, Louis was the architect of his own destruction.

By 1678 the French monarch had learned that overt aggression was not an entirely satisfactory means of achieving his aims; for the next four years he pursued a brilliantly conceived and skillfully executed policy of diplomatic and quasi-legal aggrandizement. By the treaties of Westphalia, the Pyrenees, Aix-la-Chapelle, and Nimwegen, France had acquired during the past thirty years a great number of towns and territories along her borders. Louis now announced that any territories that had in the past belonged to any of these newly acquired possessions should rightfully belong to France. A number of French courts, known as Chambers of Reunion, were established to investigate these claims, and their "findings"—inevitably pro-French—were executed by the armies of France. By a combination of this highly dubious "legal" proceeding and a judicious use of military power, Saarbrücken, Strasbourg, Luxembourg, Alsace and Lorraine (to name only the most important territories) were "reunited" into the kingdom of France. The climax of the success of this policy came in August of 1684 when the emperor Leopold, weakened by his struggle against the Turks, signed the Truce of Ratisbon (Regensburg), acknowledging French possession of all territories gained by the process of "reunion" prior to August 1, 1681. Soon, however, the fortunes of diplomacy were to turn against the Sun King.

The seizure of Strasbourg (1681), and even more the revocation of the Edict of Nantes (1685) and the subsequent persecution of French Protestants, aroused European opinion against Louis XIV as never before. Under the leadership of William of Orange, the explicitly anti-French League of Augsburg was formed in July 1686; its signatories were the emperor, the kings of Sweden and Spain, and the electors of Saxony, Bavaria, and the Palatinate. When the Glorious Revolution placed William on the English throne, England too became associated with the League, as did Holland and Savoy. Although the war which followed originally broke out over the question of the succession to the electorship of the Palatinate and the archbishopric of Cologne, it was actually fought on five fronts: the Netherlands, the Rhine valley, the Pyrenees, Savoy, and Ireland. Apart from his ambitions along the Rhine, Louis had two chief aims: to hold the territories which he had previously taken in Flanders, and to restore James II to the English throne. Considering the cost to France of ten years of war (1688–1697), his gains were at best modest. Standing virtually alone against all of Europe, he managed to retain what he had gained at Nimwegen, as well as both Alsace and Strasbourg. On the other hand, he was forced to return to Spain and the empire the vast bulk of the territories won by "reunion" and by conquest since Nimwegen; he was obliged to acknowledge William III as king of England; and he was made to renounce the claims of his candidate for the see of Cologne. Although he arrogantly claimed to have written the terms of the Treaty of Ryswick, it is clear that these very terms placed severe limitations on the ambitions of Louis XIV. The strengthened position of the emperor and the increasing unification of Protestant Europe made it almost inevitable that in the years to come his attention would be focused on the possessions of the Spanish Hapsburgs.

The succession to the Spanish throne of the sickly, impotent Charles II in 1665 had raised political and diplomatic issues of the first importance for all of Europe. By the time of the Treaty of Ryswick it was apparent to all that this mentally and physically feeble monarch had not many years to live; the inheritance of his vast territories was generally recognized as a problem that demanded an international solution. In purely dynastic terms, there were three contenders for the Spanish succession: (1) Louis XIV claimed the right of inheritance through both his mother and his wife, the eldest daughters respectively of Philip III and Philip IV, both of whom, however, had explicitly renounced all rights to the Spanish throne; (2) the emperor Leopold claimed the right through *his* mother and *his* wife who, although younger daughters of Philip III and Philip IV, had never renounced their rights; (3) Joseph Ferdinand, the electoral prince of Bavaria, put forward his claim as great-grandson of Philip IV and grandson of the sister of Charles II. In addition to the dynastic aspect of the question, however, there was the further fact that neither Holland nor England, the two great naval powers of Europe, was prepared to allow the unification of the Spanish possessions with those of France *or* the Austrian Hapsburgs. Largely for this reason, Louis XIV put forward his claim in the name of his grandson, Philip of Anjou, while the emperor claimed on behalf of his second son, Charles.

In the year 1698, while Charles II of Spain was still living, the powers of Europe met to arrange the division of his possessions upon his death. By the Treaty of Partition of that year it was agreed: (1) that the bulk of the inheritance —Spain, the Indies, and the Netherlands—would go to the electoral prince of Bavaria; (2) that Naples, Sicily, and various other Italian territories would go to the son of Louis XIV; (3) that the duchy of Milan would go to the emperor's second son, the archduke Charles. This rather highhanded proceeding enraged the dying Charles II, who thereupon bequeathed the entire inheritance to the elector of Bavaria, then a child of seven; this attempt to punish both

Louis XIV and the emperor met with the approval of England and Holland, since it tended to maintain the balance of power on the continent. No sooner had this acceptable settlement been achieved than the prince elector of Bavaria died (February 1699), opening the entire vexing question afresh. Once again negotiations among the powers were opened and, in March 1700, a second Treaty of Partition was written. By its terms, Spain, the Netherlands, and the Indies were to be given to the archduke Charles; Naples, Sicily, and the duchy of Lorraine went to the dauphin; and Milan was given to the duke of Lorraine in compensation for the loss of his duchy. With the balancing "third force" of Bavaria removed, agreement proved more difficult to achieve in 1700 than it had been in 1698. The terms of the second Treaty of Partition were rejected by both the emperor, who greedily claimed the entire inheritance for his son, and Charles II, who proceeded to bequeath all his possessions to Philip of Anjou, the grandson of Louis XIV. Louis now found himself in an odd position: he was a party to a treaty which divided the Spanish inheritance, but he was also the grandfather of the chosen heir to the entire inheritance. What was he to do? Characteristically, he decided to scrap the treaty and support the claims of Philip of Anjou. It must be added, however, that he was motivated less by the desire to gain the Spanish possessions for the House of Bourbon than by the fear that any other policy would cause Charles II to change his will and make the archduke his sole heir. Foreseeing that war with Austria was inevitable, he realistically preferred to have Spain on his side and hoped that the naval powers would remain neutral. On November 1, 1700, Charles II died and Philip of Anjou was proclaimed as Philip V of Spain. The stage was set for an international collision of unequaled magnitude.

Once again, despite his skillful maneuvers to assure the neutrality of England and Holland, Louis XIV's ambition and arrogance soon united the great powers in opposition to his designs. In February 1701 he sent French troops into the Spanish Netherlands, immediately arousing the suspicions of England and the United Provinces. His announcement that this was done simply to protect the Netherlands until Spain should be able to take over did nothing to allay these suspicions. When the French began systematically to undermine the colonial trade of England and Holland, and when Louis negotiated an alliance between Spain, Portugal, and France (June 1701), the immediate response was the formation of a Grand Alliance of England, Holland, and Austria (September 1701), later joined by Prussia, Portugal, and Savoy. Although his opposition to the Austrian Hapsburgs was originally viewed with sympathy by England and Holland, Louis had made the fatal mistake of threatening both the commercial interests of the maritime powers and the continental balance of power, which they viewed as essential to their security. During the next fifteen years France was to pay heavily for this mistake.

The War of the Spanish Succession began in 1701, with the invasion of Italy by the imperial general, Prince Eugene of Savoy. The strategy of Louis XIV was to hold the English and the Dutch in the Netherlands, while he proceeded to attack Eugene and march on to Vienna. This plan was frustrated by the great English general, the duke of Marlborough (born John Churchill), who brought his army safely from the lower Rhine to the upper Danube, where he joined Eugene in time to meet the combined French and Bavarian forces at Blenheim; the battle of Blenheim (August 13, 1704) was the first great allied victory of the war. It was soon followed by others, as the tide turned definitely against France: in Flanders, Marlborough defeated the duc de Villeroi at Ramillies (May 1706), Marlborough and Eugene bested both Vendôme and the duke of Burgundy at Oudenarde (July 1708), and, in the bloodiest battle of the war, Marlborough and Eugene won a Pyrrhic victory at Malplaquet (September 1709); in Spain, Philip V was twice driven from Madrid by British, Portugese, and Austrian forces; in Italy, an Austro-Prussian army under Eugene won a victory at Turin (September 1706) that effectively broke French power in the entire country.

By 1708, when peace negotiations began, Louis XIV was prepared to make great concessions. He was willing to recognize Charles of Austria as king of Spain, to surrender the border fortresses of the Netherlands to Holland, to restore the empire to the state prevailing at the Peace of Westphalia, and to accept the succession of Anne to the English throne. Unfortunately, the allies insisted upon one further condition: they demanded that Louis should send French armies to drive his grandson from the Spanish throne. Although virtually exhausted militarily, economically, and diplomatically, Louis still retained his pride, and this last ignominious demand proved too much for him to swallow. Rallying his people with a magnificent appeal to the glorious memories of French power, he determined to continue the war. Again in 1709, after the holocaust of Malplaquet, negotiations were opened. At this time Louis went so far as to offer to pay mercenary troops to fight against his grandson in Spain, but again the allies insisted that French soldiers should be used, and again hostilities were renewed. This time, however, the tide began to run against Louis' enemies. One is tempted to say that fate had stepped in to punish them for their arrogance, but in any case three events occurred which upset the existing political and military balance of Europe, vastly improving the position and the bargaining power of Louis XIV. In August 1710 the Whig government of England was overthrown—partly as a reaction against the slaughter of troops at Malplaquet—in the first regular and peaceful change of government under the new English party system; the Tory government that came to power was made up of Marlborough's enemies. In 1711 the archduke Charles, the allies' candidate for the Spanish throne, inherited the throne of Austria, creating a situation in which allied victory would unite all the Hapsburg territories, an event quite unacceptable to the other powers of Europe. Finally, in 1712, the French general Villars won a signal victory over Lord Albemarle at Denain. As a result of these three events, negotiations were again reopened, this time on a much more even footing.

The terms of the settlements reached at Utrecht (1713) and at Rastadt (1714) can hardly be described as a victory for either side in the war. Philip of Anjou was recognized as king of Spain at the price of renouncing all claims to the French throne and surrendering to England Gibraltar, Minorca, and certain trading rights in Latin America (the *Asiento*). The Spanish Netherlands, Milan, Sardinia, and Naples were given to Austria, despite the emperor's refusal to recognize Philip V. France ceded Newfoundland, Acadia (Nova Scotia), and the Hudson's Bay territory to England, but was allowed to maintain its frontiers intact; Louis recognized the Hanoverian succession in England and gave up his championship of the Stuart pretenders.

Certain things, however, can be said about the settlements reached at Utrecht and Rastadt. At the very least, they clearly represented the final shattering of Louis XIV's dream of European hegemony. When Louis died in 1715, his country was internally weakened to the point of bankruptcy and externally confined by the new European balance of power. It was the creation of this balance, involving all the states of Europe, and through them all the colonial areas of the world, that represented the final achievement of international politics in the seventeenth century. Wrought on the battlefields of Flanders, Germany, and Italy, this complex pattern of relations among independent, bureaucratically organized states persisted through two centuries until its destruction by the cataclysmic events of our own age.

Chronological Summary

1603–1625 Reign of James I, king of England
1604 Publication of Cervantes' *Don Quixote*
1607 Monteverdi's opera *Orfeo*
1610 Assassination of Henry IV, king of France
1610–1643 Reign of Louis XIII, king of France
1613 Galileo's *Letters on the Solar Spots*
1613–1645 Reign of Michael Romanov, tsar of Russia
1618 Outbreak of the Thirty Years' War
1620 Francis Bacon's *Novum organum*
1621 "Great Protestation" of the English Commons
1624 Richelieu comes to power
1625 Grotius' *De jure belli ac pacis*
1625–1649 Reign of Charles I, king of England
1628 Petition of Right; siege of La Rochelle; Bernini's tomb of Pope Urban VIII; Harvey's *Exercitatio anatomica*
1629 Edict of Restitution
1629–1640 Personal government of Charles I
1631 Battle of Breitenfeld
1632 Battle of Lützen
1635 Academie française founded
1637 Descartes' *Discours sur la méthode;* Milton's *Comus*

1640–1688 Reign of Frederick William, the Great Elector of Brandenburg
1642–1648 English civil wars
1643–1715 Reign of Louis XIV, king of France
1648 Peace of Westphalia
1649 Execution of Charles I, establishment of the Commonwealth
1651 Hobbes's *Leviathan*
1653 Establishment of the Protectorate; the Instrument of Government
1658 Death of Oliver Cromwell
1659 Treaty of the Pyrenees
1660 Restoration of the Stuart monarchy; Royal Society founded
1660–1685 Charles II, king of England
1661 Death of Mazarin, personal government of Louis XIV begins
1666 Molière's *Le Misanthrope*
1667 Milton's *Paradise Lost*
1668–1669 Rembrandt's "The Return of the Prodigal Son"
1670 Pascal's *Pensées*
1672–1678 Dutch War, ended by the Treaty of Nimwegen
1674 Boileau's *L'Art poétique*
1677 Racine's *Phèdre*
1678 Bunyan's *The Pilgrim's Progress*
1683 Siege of Vienna
1685 Revocation of the Edict of Nantes
1685–1688 Reign of James II, king of England
1687 Newton's *Philosophiae naturalis principia mathematica*
1688–1697 War of the League of Augsburg, ended by the Treaty of Ryswick
1688 The Glorious Revolution in England
1689 Declaration of Rights
1689 Purcell's *Dido and Aeneas*

1689–1702 William and Mary, king and queen of England
1689–1725 Peter I, tsar of Russia
1690 Locke's *An Essay concerning Human Understanding* and *Two Treatises of Civil Government*
1700–1721 The Great Northern War, ended by the Treaty of Nystadt
1701–1714 War of the Spanish Succession
1702–1714 Reign of Anne, queen of England
1707 Union of England and Scotland
1713 Peace of Utrecht
1714 Leibniz' *Monadology*

Suggestions for Further Reading

THREE volumes of The Rise of Modern Europe series, edited by W. L. Langer, cover the period 1610–1715; Carl J. Friedrich, *The Age of the Baroque, 1610–1660* (New York, 1952); F. L. Nussbaum, *The Triumph of Science and Reason, 1660–1685* (New York, 1953); and J. B. Wolf, *The Emergence of the Great Powers, 1685–1715* (New York, 1951). The first of these presents in greater detail the view of the seventeenth century that is expressed in the present volume. Of the more conventional general studies of the period, the best is still G. N. Clark's *The Seventeenth Century*, 2d ed. (Oxford, 1947), with David Ogg's *Europe in the Seventeenth Century*, 4th ed. (London, 1943), a close second. The period is also covered, albeit unevenly, by Volumes IV ("The Thirty Years' War") and V ("The Age of Louis XIV") of *The Cambridge Modern History*.

For a discussion by several authorities of the baroque as a historical, artistic, literary, and musical phenomenon, see *The Journal of Aesthetics and Art Criticism*, vol. XIV (Dec. 1955). Among the best studies of baroque art published in English are the following: Egon Friedell, *A Cultural History of the Modern Age* (New York, 1930–1932), vol. III, "Baroque and Rococo"; M. F. Bukofzer, *Music in the Baroque Era* (New York, 1947); Gilbert Highet, *The Classical Tradition* (New York, 1949).

The intense intellectual activity of the age has been treated in several excellent and stimulating volumes, some of which are happily available in inexpensive editions. Foremost among these is the late Alfred North Whitehead's brilliant *Science and the Modern World* (Mentor ed.; New York, 1952). Paul Hazard's *The European Mind, 1680–1715* (New Haven, 1952) is basic for the period. Basil Willey's *The Seventeenth Century Background* (Anchor ed.; Garden City, N.Y., 1953) attempts a synthesis of the intellectual and religious currents of the age in a manner very different from that of the present volume. A collection of excerpts from the philosophical writings of the age, with brief introductory essays, has been compiled by Stuart Hampshire in *The Age of Reason* (Mentor ed.; New York, 1959).

The literary aspect of seventeenth-century thought is developed effectively in Hershel Baker's *The Wars of Truth* (Cambridge, Mass., 1952), but the theme is the decline of Christian humanism rather than the baroque spirit and power; its emphasis is on England. The most interesting recent study of English revolutionary thought is by Perez Zagorin, *A History of Political Thought in the English Revolution* (London, 1954).

For the history of science, the relevant portions of Herbert Butterfield's *The Origins of Modern Science* (London, 1950) are recommended for a treatment that is at once sound and lucid. A. Wolf's *A History of Science, Technology and Philosophy in the 16th and 17th Centuries* (New York, 1935; Harper Torchbooks series, New York, 1959) deals with the material in an encyclopedic fashion. J. B. Conant's *On Understanding Science: An Historical Approach* (New Haven, 1947) is valuable both for the seventeenth century and for the modern study of this important field. The political implications of scientific and philosophical developments are persuasively sketched by J. E. King in his *Science and Rationalism in the Government of Louis XIV, 1661–83* (Johns Hopkins Studies in History and Political Science, LXVI, no. 2; Baltimore, 1949).

In the area where religion and social and economic life meet and interact, Max Weber's *Protestant Ethic and the Spirit of Capitalism* (tr. by Talcott Parsons; New York, 1930) and R. H. Tawney's *Religion and the Rise of Capitalism* (Mentor ed.; New York, 1954) are still exciting. A truly magistral treatment of the most important economic movement of the age is Eli Heckscher's two-volume *Mercantilism* (London, 1935). P. W. Buck's *The Politics of Mercantilism* (New York, 1942) is shorter and easier but nevertheless excellent.

Of domestic political developments in the various countries of Europe, those of England have naturally been best treated in English. In a class by itself is G. M. Trevelyan's wise and delightful *England under the Stuarts* (New York, 1904); his *The English Revolution 1688–1689* (Home University Library; New York, 1948) is also a model of historical scholarship. Apart from the monumental, multivolume history by S. R. Gardiner and the relevant volumes of the Oxford History by Godfrey Davies and G. N. Clark, the following are particularly recommended: J. W. Allen, *English Political Theory 1603–1644*, vol. I (London, 1938); G. P. Gooch and H. Laski, *English Democratic Ideas in the 17th Century* (Cambridge, 1927); F. D. Wormuth, *The Origins of Modern Constitutionalism* (New York, 1949); J. R. Tanner, *English Constitutional Conflicts of the Seventeenth Century, 1603–89* (Cambridge, 1928); Keith Feiling, *A History of the Tory Party, 1640–1710* (Oxford, 1924); and C. V. Wedgewood's two volumes, *The King's Peace, 1637–41* (New York, 1955) and *The King's War, 1641–47* (London, 1958).

For France, in addition to the volume by King mentioned above, David Ogg's *Louis XIV* (London, 1933) and J. R. Boulenger's *The Seventeenth Century* (London, 1920), a volume in The National History of France edited by Funck-Brentano, are good, if somewhat pedestrian. Aldous Huxley's study of Father Joseph, *Gray Eminence* (New York, 1941), is stimulating and beautifully written. C. W. Cole's *French Mercantilist Doctrines before Colbert* (New York, 1931), *Colbert and a*

Century of French Mercantilism (New York, 1939), and *French Mercantilism 1683–1700* (New York, 1943) are useful primarily for the sheer amount of information they contain. Hillaire Belloc's biography *Richelieu* (Philadelphia, 1929) is rather old fashioned and questionable as history, but still highly entertaining. On the whole, Maurice Ashley's *Louis XIV and the Greatness of France* (London 1948) is probably the best general work in English.

Surprisingly little of value has been written in English about central and eastern Europe during this period. Two striking exceptions are C. V. Wedgewood's *The Thirty Years' War* (New Haven, 1939) and Ferdinand Schevill's *The Great Elector* (Chicago, 1947), both of which are highly recommended for their intrinsic interest, their sound scholarship, and their literary merit. There are many general histories of Russia in English, those of George Vernadsky and Sir Bernard Pares being among the best; V. O. Kluchevshy's monumental *A History of Russia* (London, 1911–1931), although gracelessly translated, is still the classic treatment.

Index

Act of Settlement, 146
Act of Uniformity, 137
Agreement of the People (1647), 130
Agreement of the People (1649), 131-132
Aix-la-Chapelle, Treaty of, 178-179
Althusius, Johannes, 12-13, 14
Anglo-Dutch War of 1665-1667, 177
Arminius, Jacobus, 47
Asiento, 187

Bacon, Francis, 54-56, 65
Bank of England, 148
Bernini, Giovanni Lorenzo, 32-33
Bill of Rights, 145-146
Bishops' Wars, 127
Blenheim, Battle of, 185-186
Böhme, Jakob, 45-46
Boileau, Nicholas, 30
Bossuet, Bishop Jacques Bénigne, 111
Botero, Giovanni, 7
Boyle, Robert, 57-58
Buckingham, duke of, 102, 122
Bunyan, John, 31, 45
Buxtehude, Dietrich, 37

Cabal, the, 141
Calderón de la Barca, Pedro, 29

Calvinism, 48
Catholic League, 75 f.
Chambers of Reunion, 181
Charles I, 123 ff.
Charles II, 132 ff., 136 f.
Charles X Gustavus, 158 f.
Cherbury, Lord Herbert of, 71
Christian of Anhalt, 81
Christian IV of Denmark, 84
Christina, queen of Sweden, 93
Church of England, 120-121
Clarendon, earl of (Edward Hyde), 140-141
Clarendon Code, 137-138
Coke, Edward, 124
Colbert, Jean Baptiste, 3, 113-115
Conventicle Act, 137
Convention Parliament (1660), 136
Convention Parliament (1689), 144-145
Corelli, Arcangelo, 37
Corneille, Pierre, 30
Corporation Act, 137
Cortona, Pietro da, 34
Counter Reformation, 5, 6-7, 21-23
Cromwell, Oliver, 129 ff., 136
Cromwell, Richard, 135

Danby, earl of (Thomas Osborne), 141
Declaration of Rights, 145-146

Defenestration of Prague, 80
Deism, 71-72
Descartes, René, 58-62, 65, 72
Donne, John, 53
Dover, Treaty of, 138
Dryden, John, 31

Edict of Nantes, 100
    Revocation of, 117, 181
Edict of Potsdam, 157, 161
Edict of Restitution, 86-87
Elector palatine, *see* Frederick V
Eliot, Sir John, 125

Five Mile Act, 137
Franco-Dutch War, 179-180
Frederick V, elector palatine and
    "Winter King," 79 f., 81-84
Frederick William, elector of
    Brandenburg, 152, 154 ff.
Frescobaldi, Girolamo, 37
Fronde, 108-109

Galileo Galilei, 50-52, 67
Gallican Articles, 112
Gerhardt, Paul, 37
Gesù, church of Il, 32
Gongora y Argote, 29
"Gray Eminence, the" (Father
    Joseph), 25, 87-88
Great Northern War, 170-171
Great Protestation, 123
Grimmelshausen, Hans Jacob
    Christoffel von, 31
Grotius, Hugo, 14, 18, 40
Gustavus II Adolphus, 84 ff., 89 ff.

Halley, Edmund, 67
Hals, Frans, 35
Hampden, John, 127
Harrington, James, 11
Harvey, William, 56-57
Henry IV, king of France, 75

High Commission, Court of, 128
Hobbes, Thomas, 2, 14-15, 17-18,
    62-64
Holy League (1684), 174-175
Hooke, Robert, 67
Hooker, Richard, 46, 47
Huygens, Christian, 67

Innocent X, 93
Instrument of Government, 133-
    134

James I, 12, 120 ff.
James II, 142 ff.
Jansen, Cornelius, 43
Jansenism, 42-43
Jeffreys, Chief Justice, 142
Jesuits (Society of Jesus), 41 f.

Karlowitz, Treaty of, 175
Kepler, Johannes, 50, 53-54, 67

La Rochelle, 101-102
Laud, Archbishop William, 125-126
League of Augsburg, 181-182
Le Brun, Charles, 35
Leibniz, Gottfried William von,
    70-71
Leopold I, 172 ff.
Letter of Majesty (Sovereignty),
    77-78
Levelers, 130 f.
Licensing Act, 146
Lilburn, John, 5-6
Locke, John, 12-13, 15-16, 18, 71,
    139, 148
Long Parliament, 127 f., 130, 131
Lorrain, Claude, 35
Louis XIII, 98 ff.
Louis XIV, 110 ff., 175 ff.
Louvois, marquis de (F. M. Le
    Tellier), 115-116
Loyola, Ignatius of, 41
Lully, Jean Baptiste, 37

Marie de Médicis, 98
Marlborough, duke of (John Churchill), 144, 185 f.
Maximilian of Bavaria, 75-76
Mazarin, Jules, cardinal, 107-110
Mercantilism, 2 ff.
Milton, John, 27-28
Molière, Jean Baptiste, 30-31
Molina, Tirso de, 29
Monk, General George (duke of Albemarle), 135
Monmouth, duke of, 142
Monmouth's Rebellion, 142
Monteverdi, Claudio, 36-37
Murillo, Bartolomé Esteban, 35
Mutiny Act, 146

Natural Law, 13-14
New Model Army ("Ironsides"), 129 f.
Newton, Sir Isaac, 54, 67-69
Nikon, Patriarch, 163
Nimwegen, Treaty of, 180

Oates, Titus, 138
Old Believers, 163
Oliva, Treaty of, 159-160

Papists' Disabling Act, 138
Paradise Lost, 27-28
Pascal, Blaise, 43-45, 46, 57, 72
Paul V, pope, 52
Peter I ("the Great"), 152, 162 ff.
Petty, Sir William, 69-70
Pilgrim's Progress, The, 31
Poltava, battle of, 165, 170
Popish Plot, 138
Poussin, Nicholas, 35
Pride's Purge, 130-131
Protestant Union, 75 f.
Provincial Letters, 44
Pufendorf, Samuel, 15
Purcell, William, 37
Puritanism, 47

Pym, John, 127
Pyrenees, Treaty of the, 177

Racine, Jean, 31
Razin, Stenka (Stephen), 163
Reason of State, 7-8
Rembrandt van Rijn, 35-36
Remonstrants, 47-48
Reni, Guido, 34
Return of the Prodigal Son, The, 35-36
Richelieu, Cardinal (Armand Jean du Plessis), 97 ff.
Ripon, Treaty of, 127
Root and Branch Petition, 128
Rubens, Peter Paul, 34
Ruisdael, Jacob van, 35
Ryswick, Treaty of, 182

Sancroft, Archbishop William, 142-143
Scarlatti, Alessandro, 37
Scarlatti, Domenico, 37
Schütz, Heinrich, 37
Selden, John, 124
Shaftesbury, earl of (Anthony Ashley Cooper), 139
Short Parliament, 127
Siege of Vienna, 173-174
Simplicissimus, 31
Social Contract, 17 f.
Spanish Succession, 182 f.
Spinoza, Baruch (or, Benedict D'Espinoza), 15, 62, 64, 66
Star Chamber, Court of, 128
Strafford, earl of (Thomas Wentworth), 127

Test Act, 138
Three Resolutions of the House of Commons, 125
Toleration Act, 146
Tory Party, 141
Triennial Act (1641), 127

Triennial Act (1694), 146
Triple Alliance of 1668, 178
Turenne, vicomte de, 115

Utrecht and Rastadt, Treaty of, 187-188

Van Dyck, Anthony, 34
Vauban, marquis de, 115
Vega, Lope de, 29
Velasquez, Rodriguez de Silva y, 35
Vermeer, Jan, 35

Vivaldi, Antonio, 37
Vondel, Joost van den, 31

Wallenstein, Albrecht von, 85-86, 88, 90-92
War of Devolution, 177-179
War of the Spanish Succession, 185 ff.
Westphalia, Treaty (or Peace) of, 93-96, 176-177
Whig Party, 138-139
William III, of Orange, 143 ff., 179
Wren, Sir Christopher, 33, 67